"*Ordinary on Purpose* is a stunning survival tale about how to regain your footing when all feels lost, and it's proof that beauty can emerge from the ashes. The lessons humbly woven into each chapter are the reminders we all need in today's chaotic world to always seek out the extraordinary in our everyday lives. Mikala is an inspiration."

Whitney Fleming, author

lmission: Embracing a Life of Grief and Joy

"*Ordinary on Purpose* is a must-read for all women. Mikala takes us on a journey of heartbreak, forgiveness, and all the messy parts of life—and shows us there's beauty to be found in the ordinary."

Leslie Means, creator of Her View From Home

"Mikala's story is uniquely hers, yet anyone would resonate and find pieces of their journey in these pages. Her vulnerability is so powerful that you can't help but reflect on the hardship and beauty in your own life. The concept of living an 'ordinary life' will never feel the same after reading this book."

Kelli Bachara, MA, LPCC

"*This was the day I stopped pretending.* YES. In *Ordinary on Purpose*, Mikayla Albertson gives us glorious permission to live this one life without pretense or fear, and as we walk with her through her fire, at the same time we learn how to walk through our own."

Amy Betters-Midtvedt, Hiding in the Closet with Coffee

"Mikala Albertson comes to her readers as a friend with un-flinching honesty and exceptional tenderness. She brings her whole self to us so we can in turn bring our whole selves to the world. *Ordinary on Purpose* gives us permission to stop pretending and to start really living."

Jillian Benfield, author

"In *Ordinary on Purpose*, Mikala Albertson gives us permission to admit that perfect is pretend so we can finally exhale our secrets and breathe in truth. Through moving stories and with raw vulnerability, Mikala helps us to discover that the good life—the beautiful life—is right here in the ordinary."

Jenny Albers, author of *Courageously Expecting*

ordinary
on purpose

SURRENDERING
PERFECT
AND DISCOVERING BEAUTY
AMID THE RUBBLE

MIKALA ALBERTSON, MD

BETHANYHOUSE
a division of Baker Publishing Group
Minneapolis, Minnesota

© 2022 by Mikala Albertson

Published by Bethany House Publishers
11400 Hampshire Avenue South
Minneapolis, Minnesota 55438
www.bethanyhouse.com

Bethany House Publishers is a division of
Baker Publishing Group, Grand Rapids, Michigan

Printed in the United States of America

Library of Congress Cataloging-in-Publication Data
Names: Albertson, Mikala, author.
Title: Ordinary on purpose : surrendering perfect and discovering beauty amid the rubble / Mikala Albertson.
Description: Minneapolis, Minnesota : Bethany House Publishers, a division of Baker Publishing Group, 2022. | Includes bibliographical references.
Identifiers: LCCN 2021046013 | ISBN 9780764239472 (paper) | ISBN 9780764240652 (casebound) | ISBN 9781493436040 (ebook)
Subjects: LCSH: Christian women—Religious life. | Perfection—Religious aspects—Christianity.
Classification: LCC BV4527 .A39 2022 | DDC 248.8/43—dc23
LC record available at https://lccn.loc.gov/2021046013

Cover design by Brand Navigation
Cover floral image by Yaroslav Danylchenko / Stocksy

Baker Publishing Group publications use paper produced from sustainable forestry practices and post-consumer waste whenever possible.

22   23   24   25   26   27   28   7   6   5   4   3   2   1

For Dan

When my heart broke, you held a few of the pieces tightly in your grasp for a while and kept them safe. Then one day, you quietly offered those little pieces back to me. We trusted God to stitch all the pieces of us back together like a patchwork quilt . . . more beautiful than before. He took our broken hearts and our broken marriage and created a love and tenderness I never imagined. Today I'm so grateful for the things that broke me. That broke us.

It was all just a part of our becoming. Now ours is my very favorite love story. I'm so grateful to live this ordinary little life with you. I love you.

contents

PART TWO: DISCOVERING BEAUTY AMID THE RUBBLE

this ordinary life

Joy comes to us in moments—ordinary moments. We risk missing out on joy when we get too busy chasing down the extraordinary.

—Brené Brown, *Daring Greatly*

I used to think I wanted a perfect life. *Needed* a perfect life. For years I worked my tail off for it, actually. I suppose I was trying to drown out the little voice whispering in my ear for as long as I could remember, *"There is something very wrong with you."* I thought maybe if I appeared perfect enough, I'd prove that voice wrong.

Then one morning, while on hospital rounds during my family practice residency, the attending physician pulled me aside in the hall and, with worried eyes, asked, "Mikala, is everything okay?" I scanned my mind for an acceptable response. *What is it we're supposed to say?*

I hadn't been able to hide the panic from my eyes all morning. I couldn't keep my attention focused on the questions and numbers and matters at hand, on all the hurting patients right in front of my face. Because the night before, I found a black sock tucked up in the beams of our basement ceiling. My hands trembled as I unwrapped it and discovered evidence of just how bad things were with my husband. Pills and powders and other terrifying things. My mind flashed to our newborn asleep in the crib upstairs. And that next morning during rounds when the attending fixed his worried eyes on my panicked face, I longed to tell him. The truth.

I wanted to scream it, actually. "No. NOOOOO!!!! Everything is *not* okay! Everything is broken! My husband. My marriage. My life. It's all falling apart. Addiction is overtaking us!" But instead, I softly replied, "I'm fine. Sorry. I'm just . . . tired, I guess."

Ah. There it was. That's what we're supposed to say.

I didn't tell anyone about any of it.

I didn't tell anyone my husband was on drugs and my marriage was failing. I didn't mention that I was floundering through my training to become a family practice doctor and it was choking the life out of me. Or that I was struggling to hold it together for my two little boys at home. I never relayed how desperately lonely and sad and scared I was—positive I was the only one struggling. And I didn't tell a single soul that, deep down, I'd convinced myself there must be something very wrong with me.

Nope.

I didn't mention any of my painful truth to anyone.

I just smiled.

I worked a little more and pushed a little harder. I pretended. A lot. I showed up wherever I went and talked about kids or work or mom stuff or clothes or paint colors for my kitchen or how many pounds I needed to lose. The more I fumbled along through life, the nicer my clothes were, the better my hair looked, the wider my smile. And even though my life was crumbling down around my ankles, I strived *that much harder* to appear perfect.

Because isn't that what we're supposed to be doing down here? Isn't our main job on earth to attempt to live the most perfect life possible? And wouldn't anything less than perfect just seem . . . ordinary?

In truth, it felt like I was carrying a gigantic load. Picture me with six or seven or more big, heavy boxes of varying sizes, each slapped with a different label such as *Motherhood, Wifely Roles, Addict Husband, Workload, Body Image, Self-doubt, Emotional Baggage.* I stumbled around every day under the weight of this load, attempting to keep it all balanced and prevent my stack from toppling over. I made sure each box was sealed up tight so no one could see the ugly contents inside, and though I felt completely overwhelmed and exhausted and afraid and alone, on the outside I pretended things were fine. Perfectly fine!

I assumed that if I shared my real, messy, broken self with the world, people might not like me. People might judge me. People might talk about me behind my back. People might not want to be my friend. My *real* self, living this *very real* life, was too embarrassing. So every day I did my best to pretend.

Until eventually it all broke down.

My husband went to drug rehab. Again. And it became undeniably clear he was either going to get better . . . or die. Suddenly, all the boxes I was balancing came tumbling down, and my ugly truth spilled out all over the ground. In what felt like utter defeat, I dropped to my knees and began sifting. I raked through the pain and brokenness and sadness and fear and hurt and lies, and though my hands were cut and bleeding, I delicately began to pick up the pieces.

Only this time, instead of shoving my pain and brokenness back into boxes and sealing them all up tight, I chose something

11

revolutionary. I decided to *stop* pretending, and I stepped out into the world as *me*. The very real, messy, mostly ordinary me living this very real, messy, mostly ordinary life. And what happened next came softly. Slowly. Almost imperceptibly at first.

One little story, one hard truth, one authentic moment at a time, I learned to extend my hands and offer my pain and brokenness and truth for others to see. At work. In relationships. At Al-Anon meetings. Through my writing. And in return, people began trusting me with the contents of their own boxes. Now, every day I do my best to hold it all with tender hands—people's broken and sharp parts, their pieces with fraying edges, all their fear and self-doubt and guilt, their sickness and loss and pain.

During that season spent picking up the pieces, I discovered our pain and brokenness isn't something to be boxed up or hidden away. It's something to be borne. *Together*. And if we're paying attention, we'll find Jesus right there, shouldering it *all* and loving us through it, and offering grace and mercy and joy and helping us find beauty amid the rubble. Somehow, when I stopped striving and pretending, a beautiful life of connection and love and faith had room to emerge. And now I know.

"Perfect" is *pretend*.

I had been chasing the wrong thing all along! What I really want, and what I still so desperately need, is an *ordinary* life. A real, hard, lovely, ordinary life. With a sober husband and a whole herd of kids in a messy house. With days spent as a stay-at-home mom driving back and forth to school and sports and activities, then yelling at everyone to hang up their bags and put away their shoes. With a chubby tummy and tank tops and my flip-flops in our cookie-cutter house on an ordinary street in an ordinary neighborhood. With friends and church and love and neighbors and books and tomatoes in the garden and Truth and our poorly trained dog, Fern.

So this book is about that. About becoming ordinary.

I'm taking my stories out of the boxes for all to see, and the pages that follow are the story of my truth—my journey toward surrendering "perfect" in order to really *live* this good, hard, ridiculously imperfect, heartachingly beautiful, ordinary life. It's the story of becoming me. My *becoming*.

More than anything else from reading my story, I'd love to have you join me. But please know, my story doesn't mean you have to stay with your spouse. Or leave. It doesn't mean you have to quit your job or chase some new passion or have another baby or move a thousand miles away from home. This isn't a How-To book. In fact, you might find my story to be a mostly How-NOT-To guide to life. But I hope you'll see it as an invitation to stop pretending. And be *you*. Listen.

Can we tuck fear aside and unpack our truths for others to see?

Can we stop trying to carry our brokenness and pain alone and dare to ask for help?

Can we show up not as our *best*-appearing selves but as our *truest* selves?

Can we remember to pray every single day for guidance and love and support?

Can we hand our backbreaking load over to Jesus and put on His yoke instead? After all, His "burden is light."[1]

Can we silence that critical inner voice and believe we are imperfectly perfect *enough*?

Can we realize that "perfect" is *pretend* after all?

You see, every day we have a choice. We can either spend our days on this earth striving for more and pretending to be perfect, hiding all our flaws and imperfections, and never really connecting or feeling seen, or we can choose to be *real*. Then, with open arms and true love and authentic connection, maybe we can finally discover the incredible gift of a startlingly ordinary life.

And I choose *ordinary*. What about you?

Won't you grab my hand? Let's decide to live and breathe and work and love wherever God has placed us. And let's share our one precious, beautiful, *ordinary* life . . . together. I'll be me. You be you.

Come on. Let's be ordinary. On purpose.

PART ONE

surrendering "perfect"

ONE

widen the circle

As a child, my Cabbage Patch doll was a hand-sewn imitation made with so much yarn hair that she tipped over whenever I tried to make her sit on her own. "That's not a *real* Cabbage Patch!" my cousin scoffed.

I was so embarrassed.

When kindergarten rolled around, I was thrilled when my mother bought me a bright pink Cabbage Patch backpack with the half-face of a Cabbage Patch Kid and yarn pigtails sewn to the front. On the first day of school, I boarded the big yellow school bus with my empty pink, very *authentic* Cabbage Patch backpack dangling down my back. I smiled at the camera over my shoulder, feeling so proud. And I vividly remember on the last day of kindergarten rifling through that now-tattered pink backpack and pulling out my report card on the bumpy ride home from school. My eyes raced down the neat little column of boxes—A, A, A, A, A. Whew! I breathed a sigh of relief. Straight A's. Here was tangible proof I was doing life right. Perfectly, even.

Years later, at the final interview for my first real job as a family practice physician, I wore my best slacks, a ruffled floral blouse, and some pointy-toed shoes. I curled my hair in waves that framed my face and completed the outfit with a leather briefcase I had borrowed from my mom. I wanted to look professional, but that briefcase was completely empty. Still, I summoned my greatest confidence and strode into the conference room with the empty briefcase swinging by my side.

A few moments before the meeting began, the HR representative leaned over and quietly whispered, "Mikala, you should negotiate for $10,000 more."

I looked at her quizzically, and she just smiled. When the corporate guys came in to review my final contract, I asked for $10,000 more, and as I signed my name on the line, I saw the HR rep give me a small wink.

I felt just like a little girl dressed up in fancy, grown-up clothes. Just like the little girl riding home from school on a bumpy yellow bus. I glanced down at the amount written on the line in my contract and exhaled a shaky breath. Six figures. Here was tangible proof I was doing life right. Perfectly, even. I pushed the thought of my husband living in an addiction recovery house right out of my mind. Then I tucked the contract into my empty briefcase and walked away.

It seems my journey toward becoming ordinary did not progress smoothly or easily through a series of childhood life events from which I deduced important life lessons in order to learn and grow and figure out life. But rather, through a number of repeated stumbles and falls. Leaving me constantly with bloodied knees and wondering why in the world everyone else received the manual about how to do life while I was kept in the dark. Pretending. Like when you're not in on an inside joke but when everyone else laughs, you laugh too.

Growing up, what other people thought of me was absolutely essential, and I did everything I possibly could to act *just right* and follow all the rules—to fit in. But you know what the tricky part about that was? The rules seemed different everywhere I looked.

I learned very early on that teachers and parents and grown-ups really needed me to follow a specific set of rules. I suppose it made them feel better and more successful as teachers and parents and grown-ups if a child could figure out how to look just right and talk just right and act just right and appear, well . . . perfect. So, I did that. I chased perfection. But it seemed as though my peers had a whole new set of standards I needed to follow.

I attempted to blend in. Everywhere. I tried to fly a little under the radar in every single social situation. I followed whatever rules were set by whichever particular group I happened to be in at the time. I became a chameleon. The ultimate people-pleaser. I could be sporty or cheery or intelligent or sweet. And I managed to make it work. Mostly. I'm pretty sure if you asked anyone from high school or college, they'd have no idea what I am talking about. But can you relate? Writer Shauna Niequist has this to say of pushing and proving and people-pleasing in her life-giving memoir, *Present Over Perfect*:

> I've always trusted things outside myself, believing that my own voice couldn't be trusted, that my own preferences and desires would lead me astray, that it was far wiser and safer to listen to other people—other voices, the voices of the crowd. I believed it was better to measure my life by metrics out there, instead of values deeply held in my own soul and spirit.[1]

I never believed I had anything to offer. I was somehow underqualified to be the expert on even my own life. So I did everything I could to please the crowd. Everyone *outside* myself. And the truth was, I spent my entire life feeling like I was standing on the outside of a giant circle looking in.

To me, the inside of the Circle meant being beautiful and cool and popular. The inside of the Circle meant *true* belonging and represented all the things I constantly pretended to be. Every morning I left the house with the sole intention of keeping one foot inside that coveted Circle. I had the right hair. I wore the right clothes. I participated in all the right activities. And for me, nothing worked better to keep me inside that Circle than having the right friend—someone with a spot secured right in the *center* of the Circle.

I found a friend just like that in middle school. She was little and cute and outgoing and confident and bubbly. She seemed to know everyone . . . and everyone liked her. Everyone wanted to be friends with my best friend in the whole world. And I got to be her lucky sidekick.

I spent my days with her riding bikes to the pool or rolling through the Wendy's drive-through on our rollerblades. She was how I met older boys and tried alcohol and hitched rides home from the mall and went to parties where I discovered what pot smelled like. I felt eternally lucky to be her best friend. And my beautiful friend seemed to accept and love the *real* me. Plus, she made me cool.

The summer before high school, the two of us made a list of acceptable boys to date using some strict criteria (like hot, popular, older). So naturally, when Dan Albertson started calling me, I ditched my friend for him. After all, he was on our list! And he was further inside the Circle than even my adorable friend was . . . he was smart, popular, handsome, athletic, and older. He was the kind of popular kid who knew everyone's name and waved to *every single person* in the hallway. He was cool, confident, *and* kind. Plus, he could drive! Everyone liked Dan Albertson. And I got to be his lucky girlfriend.

I didn't intend to ditch my best friend. Not really. But it wasn't long before I devoted every free moment to my new boyfriend, and the closeness with my best friend sort of floated away over time. I completely ignored how much this probably hurt her, and I spent the rest of my years of high school on his arm. He made fitting into the Circle easy for me. Next to him, I didn't have to pretend. I was sure it was love. I eventually married him, so maybe it was?

Dan was the perfect accessory to my perfect life. I was a straight-A student (until that devastating B in calculus), a candidate for the prom court, salutatorian at graduation, and following my senior year, I went on a full-ride academic scholarship to the University of Nebraska at Lincoln, where I would be pre-med. All the teachers and parents and grown-ups were so happy!

On the flip side, I also rode around a lot in cars with older boys and tried pot and hung out at house parties drinking Zima and had sex with my boyfriend as a teen. Oh, and I lied. A lot. My parents almost always thought I was at the dance. All my peers were so happy!

I struck the ever-elusive balance in life. Perfect exterior. Perfect accomplishments. All while managing to please . . . everyone. But in truth, I lived with this little bit of fear and dread that one day people would notice I didn't really belong in *any* of it. I felt different. I wasn't perfect, actually. I was . . . ordinary. And I wondered constantly when everyone might realize I didn't really belong in any kind of Circle. I wondered when someone might expose the real, very *ordinary* me and shove me right out.

I couldn't wait to move on. I couldn't wait to grow up. I couldn't wait to go off to college and get my degree and marry my high school sweetheart and start my awesome career and raise my amazing family and live happily ever after. I just couldn't wait to create *my own* Circle. I was tired of following everyone else's rules. I was tired of pretending to belong. I convinced myself that when I got married and started my adult life, the Circle would somehow disappear. I was sure there would be no more pretending as a grown-up.

But the Circle doesn't really go away, does it? How disappointing to realize that, even as grown-ups, we still do our best every day to pretend we have it all together in this life. We wonder with terror when someone is going to figure us out and expose our truth to everyone. We wonder when someone will realize we don't really belong anywhere. And we struggle every day to pretend that we do! We try everything possible to keep a foot in the coveted Circle.

How disappointing to realize that, even as grown-ups, we still do our best every day to pretend we have it all together.

We strive for a well-respected career. The right hair. Trendy clothes. The fancy house (beautifully decorated, no less). Perfect prodigy children. Extravagant vacations. Family photographs in perfectly coordinated outfits (but not too matchy-matchy, of course). And every single success plastered across social media.

SEE? LOOK AT ME! I BELONG! I'M IN THE CIRCLE!

It's exhausting, isn't it? All this pretending? I mean, aren't we all just tired? Tired of smiling and faking and pretending and posturing and morphing and propping things up to look perfect??

Can I tell you something? Can I tell you what I've finally come to realize after all these years?

Around the time my marriage was dissolving—right in the middle of all my pretending and striving and attempting to have my life together and carrying around empty briefcases and trying to be perfect—I looked inside the Circle I'd spent my life striving for. I *really* looked. I peered right into the middle of that Circle with fresh eyes, and I discovered something.

The Circle is *empty*.

Seriously. There's no one inside the Circle. Not one single person.

Just like my pink Cabbage Patch backpack and the briefcase I borrowed from my mom, *the Circle is empty*.

In utter disbelief, I started looking around me and realized something else. We're all out here. On the *outside*. Everyone. *Every single one* of us is standing around out here peering in. Attempting to get one foot across the line of that stupid Circle.

Now I know, I don't have to pretend. And neither do you. Because the irony is, the *Circle* is pretend! We don't have to push and prove and prop ourselves up—hiding our messy lives, forcing our plans, and putting all our energy into pretending to be people we're not.

As Shauna Niequist has to say, "Now I know that the best thing I can offer to this world is not my force or energy, but a well-tended spirit, a wise and brave soul."[2]

Isn't that lovely?

So here's what I'm proposing.

What if we just stopped? What if we stopped putting all our force and energy into pretending to fit in and following all the rules? What if we stopped trying to fill our empty backpacks and briefcases with straight-A report cards or six-figure contracts? What if, instead of killing ourselves trying to get in, we lit the center of the Circle on fire and burned up all those ridiculous rules and expectations and lies and fake appearances? What if we decided to just be . . . ordinary?

Maybe then we could join hands and create a circle *around* that fire. And we could roast s'mores. Maybe then we could sing songs and swap real life stories and laugh and really get to know one another in our beautiful, ordinary lives. Here on the *outside* of that giant bonfire. Imperfections and all. Then, if any others want to join, we'll just open our hands to widen our circle and make some room.

Because out here, everyone belongs.

Everyone belongs.

Life becomes real and lovely and beautiful when we stop pretending and decide to live our hard, messy, very *ordinary* lives . . . together. Exactly as we are.

I don't know, I think that sounds like one heck of a party. I think that sounds like one heck of a life. Want to join me?

I'll grab the lighter.

TWO

he's waiting

I've called myself a Christian my whole life, but I'm just coming to know what it really means. I grew up going to church for the important occasions: Easter, Christmas, those sacrament years. But I didn't understand most of it. And I never really read the Bible. I tried a few times though. As a child I attempted to read it like any other book, right from the beginning. But I never got through more than a chapter or two of Genesis before I felt super bored and confused and just abandoned the whole venture for another day. Plus, our family wasn't one of those families who ever prayed together.

In third grade, my parents bought me a hamster. She was an orange, fuzzy little creature I named Harriet. Approximately two weeks after bringing my new hamster home, she had nine babies. I will never forget looking into her little white hamster house and screaming at the top of my lungs, "Mom! There's something moving in there!" Sure enough, nine hairless pink baby hamsters squirmed together in a pile. My mother was mortified. I was ecstatic!

I handled those hamsters from day one. I raked them out of their house to watch them stumble around on my hands with their little eyes closed. I attempted to feed them with a syringe. I was excited and strangely proud to watch those hairless pink bodies become covered with a fine fur. My babies were growing! Then when their eyes opened and they were eating on their own, we took them back to the pet store. Except for one.

I named him Snickers.

Because I'd been handling Snickers since the day of his birth, he was quite tame. I held him for hours every day and let him scamper up and down my arm. I designed obstacle courses out of Barbie furniture and loved to make him run around on my record player like a treadmill. I even decorated a tiny Christmas tree for him complete with homemade ornaments made of sunflower seeds and dried corn hot-glued into star shapes.

One Sunday morning, I found my pet hamster nearly lifeless at the bottom of the cage, unable to move. I'm guessing he fell from the top of his three-story cage, and when I went to pick him up, he squealed in pain. I was devastated. It was the same year I would receive First Communion because we were headed to church that day, and I spent the entire service on my knees.

Dear God, please save Snickers. Don't let him die. Don't let him die. Don't let him die.

Over and over and over I begged and pleaded for God to save my hamster. It was the first time I remember hitting my knees to pray.

But I came home to find Snickers had stopped breathing. My beloved pet was gone. I prepared my old pencil box as a casket for him with cedar chips, all his belongings, and my little grade-school picture. Then I sobbed as I buried him out back under our evergreen trees.

I felt angry. Dejected. Lonely. And ignored.

God hadn't answered my prayers. Even though I had prayed *so hard*, Snickers was gone. So I figured I was right all along. Prayers didn't matter. And God wasn't listening. Or He didn't care. Or maybe I just wasn't doing it right. I knew one thing was certain: I was alone down here. God might be for other people, but He didn't seem to be for me.

As I grew older, I never really prayerfully considered anything in my life. Not my high school boyfriend or having sex with him as a teen. Not where I would go to college or what my college major would be. Not my marriage. Not medical school or my chosen career. Not my babies. Not God's plan for my life. I never really knew how to do it. I had no idea this was a thing. Prayer? Really? I always just charged ahead through life with whatever I wanted to do or whatever I thought was best or whatever looked right at the time—or whatever the world was shouting at me from every direction. I grabbed on to other people's opinions and other people's expectations and the world's recommendations about what I should do and who I should be. *Who I was* became all tangled up in who everyone else needed me to be. And when I succeeded at fulfilling the world's expectations, well...then I didn't feel so different and alone anymore.

I tended to use God as a lifeline. I figured He was out there. Somewhere. And maybe He was listening. So I occasionally asked for help when I thought I needed it (along with very specific requests, of course). I prayed about tests and outcomes. I prayed about things that might make me look good. I prayed over things I thought would prevent failure or pain. I prayed He would fix my husband or whatever messes I got myself into.

I always figured I shouldn't really bother God. If I could go it alone, if I could manage it myself, then I should give that a try. After all, He had bigger problems to tend to. Things like world hunger and orphans and terrorists and war and chronic illness and death and failing marriages and homeless families and, you know, ALL THE OTHER PROBLEMS IN THE WORLD. He didn't have time for my little messes, right? *Right?* He wasn't paying much attention to *me*, was He? I mean, otherwise wouldn't He have saved Snickers?

It turns out, I did it wrong for about thirty-five years. And to be honest, I still struggle in this area sometimes. I'm constantly trying to do life on my own terms. And I'm guessing God smiles at me a lot. I bet He is constantly giving me the look I give my kids. Not the impatient one. Not the huffing-in-exasperation, rolling-my-eyes-to-the-ceiling look that says "Ugh. Seriously?" No, not that look.

The one that says, "You are so cute! That's hilarious. I just love you soooo much even though you have it so perfectly wrong." It's the same look I give my daughter as I wait patiently for her to put on her own outfit or move the wet clothes from the washer to the dryer or painstakingly unload every glass from the top rack of the dishwasher. The look that says, "I know you'll get it eventually, I'll wait," while I stretch out my hand for whenever she needs me or for when she's ready to receive a triumphant hug.

Every single day right in the middle of an ordinary life, God stands right here beside us with His hand outstretched.

Every single day right in the middle of an ordinary life, God stands *right here beside me* with His hand outstretched. Waiting. Waiting for me to stop grabbing at everything and clutching for control. Just waiting for me to hand it over. Again. Because He is God. He can carry it all. The big *and* the trivial.

And I don't have to hold it all so tight.

28

Looking back, I think my marriage was excruciatingly hard for a reason. I think my medical training and years in residency nearly broke me for a reason. I think I felt so deeply and cried so often over other people's stories for a reason. That's how God found me. That's how He finally drew me back. I hadn't been listening all those years. I refused to talk to Him or share my life with Him. So God started ever so gently . . . SHOUTING.

"My darling! Why won't you talk to me?! Why won't you give this to me? Why won't you let me carry this for you—your pain, your sadness, your fear, YOU?? Why won't you listen? I care about all of it! The good, the bad, the miniscule, the ordinary! I'm here! You don't have to carry it all on your own. Lay it down, honey! Come follow me! I LOVE YOU. I just want YOU!! You don't have to be afraid . . . I'm here! Stop grabbing and clutching and clawing for control. I'm right here, sweetheart! Just LET GO!"

A few years ago, I became more serious about my faith. I started thinking about my purpose and this life and what it all means. I began going to church regularly. I started reading the Bible. *Really* reading. I had heard it all before in bits and pieces, but I just hadn't realized it applied to *me*. And I'm still shocked sometimes. Isn't it amazing? He means *me*! Now I read a verse and think, *Wow. There's some really great stuff in here! It's almost like a How-To Guide to Life. Who knew?*

I feel so late to the party.

And I never intended to write about it. I never in a million years imagined submitting a book to be shelved in the Christian Living section of the bookstore. Sometimes I feel totally unqualified to share the gospel. I feel like a beginner. A newbie. An infant in my faith. My eyes are freshly opened. I am exactly like the people waiting on the other side of the lake who

29

were finally awakened by Jesus' miraculous signs in John 6:25: "Rabbi, when did you get here?"

It feels like I've woken up for the very first time. And I finally realize, *He was with me all along. I was never, ever alone one single day in my life. I was beloved. Every single second. Every single breath.* It makes me want to talk about it. About Him. It makes me want to be a good person. Not for the accolades of anyone down here. Not in an attempt to win His love—He already loves me! I just want to bring praise and glory to God.

I know I have so much to learn. I probably still get it wrong half the time. I mess up a lot. I sin. I'm sure I misinterpret verses. I struggle with a shaky faith. So often I still have to remind myself, *He comes first.* And He wants me to share my life with Him. My *real* life. Every bit. He is the only one who matters, after all.

Because one day all the rest will be stripped away. All the ways I define myself will be gone. Mother. Wife. Doctor. Writer. Sister. Daughter. Friend. Those sticky labels will be picked and peeled away. My awards and accomplishments will vanish. All the things I've so carefully and painstakingly added to my life's résumé to prove I am good will be erased. Gone in an instant.

And one day I'll stand there in front of Him completely alone. Bare. Stripped even of my earthly body. My face. The dimple in my right cheek. My hazel eyes. Perhaps just a shimmering image of my soul holding my heart in my shimmering hands.

I wonder if He'll still recognize me? Will He recognize me right away because of who I am . . . in Him? If the only way to tell who I am, my truest self, is to crack open my now-exposed heart to see what's inside, will the fruit of the Spirit come pouring out? Will He see my goodness and kindness and faithfulness? Will He see my love and joy and peace and patience? Without all my labels and titles and accomplishments to prove *who* I am . . . will He know me?

Will His face light up with a smile as He proclaims, *"Oh, yes, my daughter! There you are. Of course, sweetheart. I've been waiting! Now, where were we? I think you were just telling me something about your son?"* Or will He simply squint His eyes and stare? Then turn away as He whispers, *"I never knew you"* (Matthew 7:23).

I want my God to *know* me.

And I'm getting better at praying now. After all these years, I'm getting better at constant conversation and constant contact with God right in the middle of a perfectly ordinary day. I probably still don't do it right. I just talk and cry and babble without much rhyme or reason. But something tells me He doesn't care about the words I use. He's been waiting for so long and He's just happy to have me share my life with Him. He's just happy to hear my voice. To *know* me. And He wants me to keep showing up. Keep learning. Keep repenting and serving. Keep raising my hand. Keep accepting His ridiculous grace. My heart is His. *His.* I am chosen, and that's all I need to know.

I guess my point in telling you all this is, I'm in my forties. God waited a looooong time with His hand outstretched. Waiting. For *me*. And it's never too late. Ever. He's waiting for *you*. He chose you too, beloved.

And maybe God doesn't show us who He is the way we always imagined He would—with a deep voice booming from the sky or a yes answer to everything our hearts desire. Maybe we find Him in our prayers. In our hopes and dreams. In our deepest passions. Maybe He shows up in what we're good at or in the people we are asked to love every day. Maybe He is in the risks we take. Or perhaps He meets us in our fears. Maybe He's right there in the middle of an ordinary Tuesday as we wash breakfast dishes or switch laundry from the washer to the dryer. And maybe we need to let go of chasing perfection

. . . and seek only to find *Him*. Maybe God's plan for our lives is that we stop chasing and fretting and stewing and searching for His "plan" and just love Him—our perfect God right in the middle of our messy, ordinary lives. And maybe when we unclench the fists we've wrapped so tightly around being perfect, we'll truly begin to *live*.

In Him.

Let's bring it all to Him . . . our troubles, our failures, our hopes, our fears, our beautiful, messy lives. We don't have to have a perfect faith to give Him every little piece of our hearts and follow Him.

He's waiting. And He feels like coming home.

I know that now.

But *a lot* had to happen before I knew.

THREE

we'll do it right

Aren't we all just out here, gathering clues, trying our best to
hit the mark on love and belonging?
—Shannan Martin, *The Ministry of Ordinary Places*

I hadn't planned on cockroaches. I hadn't planned on my husband's alcohol and drug addiction as we struggled through our first years of training to become doctors together either. But just a year or so after we were married, I was dealing with both.

I had hoped getting married would fix my constant need for pretending. On my wedding day, I remember keeping my eyes focused on my soon-to-be husband's face at the end of the long aisle. I felt so safe and seen in his familiar, kind eyes as I thought to myself, *I have loved you my whole life. Now this is it. The beginning. The first day of . . . forever. It's finally happening. We're an US.*

Mr. and Mrs. Dan and Mikala Albertson.

I couldn't wait for our happily ever after to just hurry up and get started already. A dream house and our successful careers and perfect kids and beautiful holidays and a loyal dog. The whole works. I could feel our perfect little plan right at my fingertips. So we commenced playing house.

We unwrapped all the dishes and towels and serving spoons and bedsheets and twelve place settings of platinum china from our wedding guests and set everything up in our first little apartment complete with hand-me-down furniture and a teeny, tiny double bed. We bought an entertainment center at a garage sale for thirty dollars, and by the time we drove it home, it was listing so severely to the left, I was sure it would collapse any minute. I cooked us fancy dinners from a box. We made love. We called the landlord to have him spray for the unwelcome little houseguests we found in the shower or hiding in corners or scrambling next to the baseboards on the floor. And we were happy. Mostly. Except occasionally during those first years of marriage, every once in a while, I'd catch my husband in a lie.

He smokes? How did I never know that? And where the heck IS he, anyway? Why didn't he call to check in? Does he think he can just show up willy-nilly, whenever he feels like coming home? Doesn't he know I am going to lie awake and worry? Doesn't he care?? We are married now, so we are one. Why doesn't he know how to behave like a husband? Couldn't he at least pretend? I am so good at pretending! I have been pretending most of my life, in fact. He should just do what I do!

I lectured about all these things. I shot withering glances and punished with my very best silent treatment. I yelled so loud the little v-shaped vein in my forehead swelled to a deep, pulsating purple. I cried. A lot. And I lost sleep. A lot. I practiced up on my martyr complex. And I'll never forget the first time I watched him pour a gas-station super-sized cup of rum and Coke one Sunday afternoon. As my scathing stares and righteous lectures began, he turned to me and declared, "I'm not going to be an alcoholic, okay?"

Well.

Okay then.

And suddenly the occasional lecture and the occasional lie and the occasional yelling match and the occasional silent treatment became the standard for our relationship.

This was not what I signed up for. This was not a marriage. This was not the happily ever after I had always imagined. But I had no idea what I was supposed to do about it. So I just kept pretending.

I pushed harder and gripped tighter.

I held on with all my might.

Then I wore a midriff when I dropped him off at rehab the first time. I actually *planned* outfits for my two-night stay. Because for me, that first trip to rehab down in Norton, Kansas felt like a bump in the road. A little blip in the timeline. A minor derailment. On the way there, we stopped to spend an afternoon walking through the archway museum in Kearney, Nebraska, like we were on vacation or something. And when we arrived, the man who would be Dan's counselor let his eyes rest briefly on my exposed waistline as he quipped, "Wow. This is your *wife?*" then handed us a clipboard full of paperwork. Looking back, I think he was slightly amused.

At the time, I assumed we'd just figure it out. We'd do all the right things. We'd get back on track. We'd follow all the rules and BOOM, problem solved. We'd just be *compliant*.

I was so good at that! I spent most of my life attempting to be compliant. Because of the plan, of course. Remember the plan? The *perfect* plan I'd been crafting for years? To me, it all seemed simple enough. Do all the right things and get the desired results. I had been on this track for so long. I was a good girl. A smart kid. A rule-follower. A people-pleaser. *Oh good, there's an instruction manual for this? A How-To in Twelve Easy Steps?*

Great! I'm in! Just tell me what to do! I'll do it! And as a result, I had a pretty impressive résumé. I was known for doing the right things. And it worked out pretty well . . . for a while. I finished college, got accepted to medical school, and married the boy.

To tell you the truth, I was actually a little relieved when Dan got into some pretty serious trouble during medical school and was forced into rehab for thirty days. Because *surely* rehab would do it. I had already tried everything I could think of and exhausted every possible effort attempting *all* the things to fix us. Following and checking and counting and lecturing and begging and praying and fighting and belittling and pleasing and threatening. All the while pretending. We hadn't been anywhere near the track toward our "plan" for quite some time. But surely *this* would get our marriage and the perfect little life I always wanted right back on the rails.

While he was gone those first few weeks, I bought tons of the Al-Anon literature the rehab facility recommended. I was looking for the perfect How-To (How To Fix Your Broken Husband, How To Fix Your Broken Marriage, How To Get the Perfect Life You Always Dreamed About). I went to medical school lectures all day, and then every evening I completely devoured Al-Anon books and daily meditations for those living with addiction in the family. I figured I could get through all of the Big Book (the main Al-Anon textbook) while he was away. I'd pound out those twelve steps in no time! *JUST TELL ME WHAT TO DO AND I'LL DO IT! I'll be sooooo compliant!*

When I visited him in rehab a few weeks later, I enjoyed the meetings and small groups, of course. It was all very informative. The counselors shared some really head-scratching truths. But I was pretty sure we weren't the type of people who belonged there. Not really. Everyone else seemed to be really, well . . . struggling. Broken homes. Broken marriages. Bankruptcy. Chronic disease. Homelessness. Missing teeth. Jail time. IV drug use. Broken lives. None of those things were *our* problems. I mean, after a few more years of medical school and three years of residency training, we were going to be doctors. Then we could begin our *amazing* life. We just needed a little help to get us back on course, right? We had a plan!

I'm embarrassed to say there was a brief moment when one night during my stay, I found myself lying next to my husband in that run-down 1970s motel-turned-rehab facility with a dirty, rust-colored brocade chair in the corner and a dingy, mustard bedspread at our feet wondering, *Would it be weird if we went ahead and tried for a baby anyway?*

In rehab.

Because according to my master plan, we were ready for a family. You know, married three years. Mid-twenties. Plus, I think I was ovulating. I didn't want to miss the chance! Never mind that our marriage and my husband and our life were a *mess*.

Clearly, I was out of my mind!

Unfortunately, it went on that way for a while. For years, actually. Through relapse (almost immediately, no surprise). Through the birth of two babies and several years of my family practice residency. Through so many tears. So many fights. So many lies and one plate hurled across the kitchen that shattered on the floor and lots of financial debt and then eventually my silent retreat into my own quiet corner. It went on through basically a complete and total destruction of my so very carefully crafted plan.

The plan was broken. Our marriage was broken. I convinced myself I must be broken too. And finally. Finally! FINALLY! I realized compliance wasn't the answer.

Because compliance means working hard, following all the rules, always doing things by the book, persisting until we can be certain we are doing life *right* . . . but feeling riddled with anxiety and stress and people-pleasing and guilt and absolute fear of failure.

Compliance means holding tightly to every single thing in our lives and trying to make it all go *our way*. Never mind what others in our family need. Never mind what is best for our marriage. Never mind which way God seems to be leading. Never mind what feels good and right and whole deep down in our *souls*.

Compliance means sticking with "the plan" no matter what. And worrying about what other people think and what other people want and what everyone might say. It's believing every single thing the people *outside* of ourselves tell us about who we are supposed to be and how our lives are supposed to look. Even when it all contradicts! Then absolutely killing ourselves attempting to make it so.

Compliance is constantly fumbling and clutching and clawing for control. Pushing harder. Gripping tighter. Making certain we are perfect. Or at least appearing to be. And compliance means continually asking of God, *Why? Why me? I'm doing ALL the right things. Why isn't my life working according to MY plan? Where are you, God?!?*

Compliance is totally and completely 100 percent exhausting. And it certainly isn't sustainable.

Finally, one day in utter defeat, I admitted to myself that compliance wasn't working for me anymore. It probably never did. This way of living left me broken. My husband was broken. Our marriage? This life plan? All completely broken.

You want to know Al-Anon's Step One?

"We admitted we were powerless over alcohol—that our lives had become unmanageable."

Yep. That sounded absolutely right. *Unmanageable* was exactly the right word to describe my family. My husband. My plan. And my *life*. With enough pain and brokenness, we become willing to change.

FOUR

i am not alone

The LORD your God will be with you wherever you go.

Joshua 1:9

I fully believed somehow motherhood would fulfill me.

For so many years I spent my time and energy placing any and all expectations for love and life and belonging in the hands of other people. Or my life's circumstances. Or things and places and events *outside* myself. Growing up, those hands belonged to my mom, then my high school sweetheart who eventually became my husband, followed by my aspirations for a fulfilling career and a perfect life.

Motherhood was next on the list.

I was the little girl who played with dolls a little too long, and I always felt that high school, college, even medical school were just a prelude to what I really wanted, what I was meant for: being a mom.

Oh, how I wanted a baby. I wanted a family. I wanted what I saw on TV commercials or what I read about in Hallmark cards or what I saw at the movies as part of every love story.

A baby made perfect sense to me. It seemed as though that's what we were supposed to do next as a young married couple. *And maybe with a baby,* I reasoned, *our little life would start looking and behaving like everyone else's in the world.*

Maybe *this* would be it. Maybe *this* would be everything I ever wanted. I felt confident motherhood would be my place to shine.

I bought a floor-model crib on clearance months before we began formally "trying," although I knew deep down it was a terrible idea. Things were going from bad to worse at home. But I wanted so badly to be a mother. I wanted a family. I *knew* this was for me.

It had to be.

But trying for a baby did absolutely nothing to fix my husband's problem with addiction, and that clearance crib looked so lonely and forlorn leaning against the wall of our bedroom in pieces while he was away at rehab. The little dream of the beautiful family I carried in my heart seemed so very far away for a while. Then after thirty days, when he came home from the inpatient treatment facility, he seemed okay. At first. And I began to lie sweetly to myself once again. He was fine. We were fine. It was all going to be fiiiiiine.

Soon after that, we moved into a charming little two-bedroom house settled in a nostalgic tree-lined neighborhood on Poppleton Street near the Nebraska Medical Center in downtown Omaha. It was white with black shutters and an adorable turquoise front door. The original hardwood floors gave welcoming creaks and groans every few steps, and wide baseboards and bright white arches separated every room. I loved the big, heavy doors with those dainty antique-glass knobs and the old coal chute in the basement. And I completely adored how everything about this house was small. Teeny-tiny kitchen. Living room with barely enough room for a couch. Two dinky little bedrooms. In my eyes, our itty-bitty, charming old home was perfect! And so happy. And *ours*. I was delighted to find initials carved into the concrete foundation on the laundry room floor next to a date from 1921. The inner romantic in me imagined it was probably their first real home too.

I painted every room a different shade of sweet pastel: turquoise and yellow and lavender and green. I handwashed our dishes because there was no dishwasher, and I hung the clothes on the line because, in the beginning, there was no plug for the dryer. I loved to throw the kitchen windows open wide to take in the smell of the gigantic lilac bush growing right outside. Then every night when I wasn't on call at the hospital, I sat in the corner of the second bedroom on my little thrift-store rocker daydreaming about the baby we would bring home one day.

Soon.

Because after six unsuccessful months of trying, just two weeks after we moved into our new house and the same month I began my first year of residency training, I stood in the bathroom one Sunday afternoon with shaking hands. To my absolute surprise and utter delight, two little blue lines appeared on the white stick I was holding, and tears sprang instantly to my eyes. My heart fluttered as my breath caught a little in my throat.

A baby.

We're having a baby.

I expected to feel a little glimpse of happily ever after for our family, but that's not exactly what I felt in that beautiful moment. Instead, for the first time in my entire life, those two little blue lines whispered so very quietly I almost couldn't hear it, *"You are not alone."*

Those two lines told me it was no longer me against the world or me trying to fit into any Circle or me attempting to survive a broken marriage or me carrying a load of heavy boxes

all taped up so no one could see the ugly truth inside. It was me
. . . and my *baby*. Me, as *mom*. And the two of us (okay, and
my husband) beginning a new life in our happy little home.
Those two lines told me I wasn't alone down here anymore.

Over the next nine months, I spent my evenings rocking in
the nursery rocker, singing softly to the baby kicking in my
belly. Pulling out tiny blue onesies to hold up against my growing tummy. Folding and refolding those tiny sleepers. Staring
around our adorable little nursery and trying to memorize every
detail. Opening the Johnson's baby lotion for a good, long
whiff. Holding itty-bitty newborn diapers softly between my
fingers. And trying to imagine what it might be like to have an
actual baby.

My baby.

Then came the day when this perfect, gentle little bundle
melted into my arms, and everything about my life changed.
Time stood still. Suddenly none of the other problems in my life
mattered except that moment. Right there. With him. I wasn't
thinking so much about perfection or attaining or achieving
or striving. I could only feel *love*. Beautiful and pure. My im-
mediate love for him was like everything and nothing I could
have imagined. This was the very first day.

Motherhood stretched endlessly before me.

I remember exactly how his face looked. How he smelled.
I remember the feeling of wrapping my palms gently under
his fragile arms and around his little ribcage and lifting his
scrunched-up ball of a body to my bare chest and snuggling
him into my neck. My hands have the *exact* muscle memory
of encircling my long fingers around his tiny wrists and ankles. I remember examining his toes. The sound of his cry.
The smacking sound of his lips. The gentle in and out of his
breath. How raw and delicate it all was. I remember thinking,

He lives! I had never loved one single thing in my life more than I loved my brand-new baby boy. I couldn't pull my eyes away.

Despite the mess of my life, God chose the perfect day, the perfect time in my life, the perfect *moment* to make me a mommy. And as I gazed upon my baby's beautiful little face, in that instant, I knew I would spend the rest of my life loving him. Giving to him. Teaching him. Showing him the world. And doing everything in my power to give him a good life.

> *I knew without a doubt there are parts of this messy, ordinary life that are indeed lovely. And holy. Perfect in their own way.*

That day I knew without a doubt there are parts of this messy, ordinary life that are indeed lovely. And holy. Perfect in their own way. Moments created by God just for me. Motherhood was absolutely *meant* for me. I was holding a child. *My* child. Isaiah was meant for me. He was the only one who'd ever been so close to my heart. A part of me, even. Now right here in my hands. I felt like I knew everything about him. I had carried his every heartbeat. Here was a whole new person born of my womb. He was *mine*. And I was his mother.

I remember later wondering why I didn't have the same visceral response to the birth of my other children. I loved them instantly. Fully. Completely. Just like a mother does. But when my other children were born, time didn't stand still as it did with my first. Magical. Holy. And I realize now it wasn't because of the baby. It was about *me*. Having my first baby and holding him in my arms was the exact moment a *mother* was born. I came blinking my eyes against a great light. Stretching my lungs. Deepening my breath. Wondering about this new place. This whole new world I'd been born into . . . motherhood.

There was a time before I became a mother, and now there is an after.

I have never, ever been the same.

But honestly?? I was wrong in the bathroom, you know. It took me a while, but I eventually realized I had it wrong all along. The quiet assurance of those two little blue lines in the bathroom that day had nothing to do with the baby. A baby wouldn't be able to carry any of my expectations or fulfill me. He was so little. So perfect. I couldn't hand him that burden. It wouldn't be fair. The day I became a mother was the moment I began to understand, for the very first time, I could not do motherhood on my own. I could not do *life* on my own. And it was during this season I *really* began to pray.

God, help me do this. I need help. I need you, Jesus.

Those two lines on my pregnancy test had whispered so quietly, *"You are not alone."* But they weren't talking about the baby. No, they were whispering of Jesus. He goes with me. Always. And He can carry it *all*.

Once upon a time, I became a mother. And with a baby in my arms and Jesus by my side, I realized, for the very first time, I wasn't alone down here anymore.

The truth is, I never really was.

FIVE

surrender

Coming home will always be the best part of going to work. And coming home to my baby was the *best* part of overnight call at the hospital during those long years of residency. I always counted down the hours and minutes, even seconds, until I could snuggle his chubby body, smell the top of his soft head, and curl up for a nap with him on our bed. It was the only thing that got me through, actually. Day after day, my baby saved me.

Then one morning, after a thirty-hour overnight call shift, I came home a few minutes early to find my husband and my baby in the kitchen. Isaiah, about nine months old at the time, sat in the highchair shoveling Cheerios into his mouth and playing with a spatula while Dan unloaded groceries. And I don't think they expected me home quite so soon.

"Hi, guys! Hiiiiii, baby! I miiiiiissed you!" I called out, drawing out the vowels in a singsong voice as I swung my overnight bag to the floor and sighed. Coming home was *always* a sigh of relief.

Except on this day.

On this day, as I smiled and cooed at my sweet baby in his highchair, my eyes drifted down to the kitchen countertop and settled on a fine powder arranged in perfect long lines, squared up neatly with the edges of a credit card alongside a rolled-up five-dollar bill. Just like in the movies.

Wait. What was this? What the HELL was this?

I knew drugs were becoming more of a problem for my husband, but *was he doing drugs while in charge of a baby? RIGHT IN FRONT OF THE BABY? Our BABY?*

And suddenly it all came out. All my pain. All my fear. All the bitterness and resentment I'd been storing away for years. All my exhaustion. I was *so* tired and *so* worn out and *so* angry. I exploded.

"What's all *THIS*???"

He turned and stared at me. Surprised.

"Just what do you think you're doing right now?"

He shook his head and looked away. "Mikala . . . stop."

My voice escalated. "You're doing drugs in front of the *baby*? What are you thinking?!"

My face turned to disgust as I stared incredulously at this scene.

My baby.

My husband.

The highchair.

That disgusting powder.

He looked back. "Mikala, just STOP. I don't need this. I'm tired. I've been up with him all night. I don't need you to walk in and start with this already."

"Well, I don't really care. I don't need *THIS*! You think I want to work all night and know that my baby is home with a father who thinks it's okay to do *drugs*? Right in front of him? A *baby*?? YOU'RE SUPPOSED TO BE TAKING CARE OF A BABY!! What kind of a father does that??"

"He's little. He doesn't even know."

I gave a sick laugh, and my voice dripped with accusation. "Yeah. He's little *now*. Don't you think he's watching? Is this really what you want for him? When will this stop?? When he's one? Two? Is this *ever* going to stop? Don't you think he's going to know his dad is on drugs?? Do you really want him to *know*??"

At this point I started screaming, "IS THIS REALLY WHO YOU WANT TO BE??"

My voice cracked. Hot tears burned at my eyes as I screamed so hard and so loud my own ears rang, and I thought my temples might explode.

I dissolved into angry, out-of-control sobs. I bawled and wailed and cried.

"I can't do this! I REALLY CAN'T DO THIS!! I don't want this! I HATE this!!! I DON'T WANT ANY OF THIS!!!" And with each word, I moved closer and closer to him.

My voice had reached hysteria. "I HATE THIIIIIS!!!"

"Just stop it, okay? You have got to STOP!!"

But I didn't stop. I couldn't stop. I started beating his chest with my fists.

"THIS! IS! NOT! A! MARRIAGE!!!"

Beat, beat, beat, beat, beat.

I hated him. Loathed him in that moment. *How could he do this to me? How could he do this to our baby? And our life?? How could he ruin everything? How???*

"STOP IT!!! WHAT ARE YOU DOING? STOP IT RIGHT NOW!!!" he shouted as he pushed my hands away. "IT'S ENOUGH!!! MIKALA! STOP!!!"

But I couldn't stop. I pressed every button I could think of. I shouted every awful, hateful thing that slammed into my mind. Everything I'd been holding back came clawing out of my mouth. I wanted him to feel bad. I wanted him to feel ashamed and small and . . . worthless. I wanted him to be as angry as I was. I wanted him to feel the same searing pain constricting my chest and piercing my heart until it felt like I couldn't breathe.

And it worked.

With intense pain and anger in his eyes, he leaned forward. "YOU THINK YOU'RE SO PERFECT? YOU THINK I WANT THIS? THIS MARRIAGE?? YOU ARE ACTING CRAZY!! STOOOOP!!!"

But I just continued screaming and pounding. "THIS!! IS!! NOT!! A!! LIFE!!!"

Pound, pound, pound, pound, pound.

He caught my wrists now in his hands. Trying to maintain composure. Trying to stop me. Trying to hold my arms down and stop the hysteria by shouting, "MIKALA, STOP!!! JUST STOOOOOOP IT!!!"

Then my excruciating pain completely overtook me as I pushed my face so close to his that our noses were nearly touching, and I screamed as loudly and desperately and frantically as I possibly could.

"JUST HIIIIIIT ME!!! COME OOOOOON!! DO IT!! JUST DOOOO IIIIT!!! HIT ME!! HIT MEEEEEEEE!!!"

I wanted him to punch me in the face. I wanted him to knock me down. I wanted him to beat me and leave me bloodied on the floor. I was in so much pain. I only wanted more pain. I wanted my body to physically feel exactly the way my heart was hurting. I wanted *pain*. Awful, unbearable, life-crushing pain. And I wanted a reason to leave him. I wanted a reason to gather up our baby and walk away and never see his face again. I wanted to leave all this pain behind. Forever. I believed if he was ever physically abusive, then I would finally have a good and tangible reason to leave. It was the *only* reason I could think of for leaving.

But he didn't. He didn't move. His eyes flashed with anger, and I recognized that same searing pain. But he didn't lay even the tiniest little finger on me. He just held my arms away from his chest. And he never, ever hurt me that way.

I can see it now in his eyes when I think back. . . . his pain was even greater than mine because it was from self-inflicted wounds. The very most painful kind. He hated himself more than I hated him in that moment. He was already beaten and bloodied on the floor. And he had done it to himself. I know that now.

Then, just as suddenly as it all began, it stopped.

Oh my God. My baby.

I snapped back to reality as my heart sank. I turned to our terrified baby boy who had dropped the spatula to the floor as he sat trapped in the highchair watching this awful scene. He was screaming too. I whisked him up out of the highchair and off to our green rocker in the living room to the sound of my husband slamming the back door.

And I knew. In that gut-wrenching moment I knew, *knew* in my heart this would never happen again. It could never happen again. I had a baby now. A whole little person I was responsible for. It was my job as his mother to keep him safe and happy and healthy and warm. I was his safe space. His soft place. His mother. Home.

I had scared my own baby, my treasure. My *love.*

"I'm so sorry, baby. I'm so sorry we scared you. It's okay. I'm here. I'm so sorry. I'm sorry. I'm sorry, baby. Oh, God. I'm sorry," I whispered over and over and over.

This was the moment I retreated.

We would never fight like that again.

Never.

We argued on occasion, yes. But never more than a raised voice here or a sarcastic slight there. Instead, I became bitter. And angry. I huffed. I rolled my eyes. I gave passive-aggressive replies. I silently seethed. And for the longest time we moved quietly past one another through this life.

Never again.
I retreated in silence. Off to my own little corner.

Until things got worse.
My husband's using increased until it became commonplace for him to either be high and running around like the Energizer Bunny, or so slow and sleepy that he slurred his words. I did my best to compensate. For example, I developed this habit of keenly evaluating his eyes on our way to the car and declaring with certainty, "I'm driving!" almost everywhere we went.

Life was a long and steady deterioration.

I continued through my final years of residency. Somehow, Dan began his first year of residency to become a pathologist. We had another baby, Eli, my heart's next great love. And I watched helplessly as my husband slowly and silently slipped further away. Away from me. Away from our family. Away from life.

Finally, there came a time I was convinced he was going to die.

I'm not trying to be dramatic; I just don't want to sugarcoat it. *He was going to die.*

Drugs and alcohol had grabbed ahold of this man I'd loved my whole life—my high school sweetheart, my husband of seven years, the father of my two children—and with its razor-sharp claws, addiction pulled him under. The kind, confident man I once knew was gone. Lost in the darkness. Stumbling and broken and ashamed and alone. He was trapped. And he was struggling for air. He was going to die.

I waited for the day I'd find him unresponsive at home. Waited for the day I'd discover he'd killed himself. Waited for the day I'd get a phone call from the hospital explaining he was in a car accident. I would've been devastated, of course, but not surprised.

It was the bottom for my husband. And our marriage.

This was the bottom for our little family.

And that bottom felt like a gigantic dark pit. The scariest dark pit imaginable. As deep as the Grand Canyon. And as wide across too. And dank and musty and cold. All I could make out down there in the dim light of that pit were giant bottles of pills from God knows who that were completely emptied in just a day or two. Plus hard liquor hidden in the garage, endless lies, thousands of dollars in credit card debt I wasn't even aware of, aluminum cans fashioned into pipes tossed out in the backyard, gambling binges and felony charges for writing fraudulent prescriptions, five years of probation to keep his medical license, and continual heartbreaking pain. So much pain. It was a pit of terrifying pain down there at the bottom.

Rock bottom.

And the hardest part about it was, we were down there together, my husband and I, but we couldn't find each other in the dark. The bottom of that pit was so big and so deep and so wide. Sometimes I called out to him, and I think he heard something. But his voice in return sounded so far away. I couldn't find him. I couldn't go to him. I couldn't reach him. We just fumbled around down there in the dark. Each of us completely alone.

I caught a glimpse of him from time to time and was shocked by his appearance. I noticed he had lost about twenty pounds. I noticed his face was covered in pick marks and scabs. And he smelled like chemicals and poison were sweating out through his pores. He couldn't seem to hold his arms still, and his hands had a fine tremor. He never really slept. And his eyes looked vacant. And lost. Then, just as soon as I'd catch a glimpse of him in our rock bottom, he'd be gone. And though he stood right before my very eyes—shared my bed, even—he'd be off on his own. Carrying his shame like a heavy load on his back. Fumbling through that terrifying pit alone, with his hands outstretched in the dark.

I tried everything. Everything. I promise, I tried absolutely *everything* to heal him. To help our marriage. To save our little family. Yelling. Fighting. Arguing. Reasoning. Loving. Crying. Begging. Guilting. Being unreasonable. Blaming. Counting pills. Following him. Checking up. Making excuses. Ignoring it. Praying. Pretending. Growing silent.

I thought, *Maybe if I'm just more available? More loving? Maybe if we have sex more? Maybe if I just keep pushing us forward through life? Maybe if I just carry him? Maybe once we finish school? Maybe once we start a family?*

But no. Nothing worked. No matter what I tried, I couldn't pull him out. I couldn't bring him back into the light. It was so incredibly painful to realize *I could not save him.* I was powerless. And the heartbreaking reality was, he never could see me down there with him in that pit. He didn't know I was there with him at the bottom. He thought he was all alone for years.

Seven years.

And I was just waiting, really. He was going to die from this disease. He was going to die . . . seemingly all alone.

I waved my white flag in weary surrender one night at the hospital after I finished several admissions in the ER. I had been awake for nearly twenty-two hours. And as I plodded down the deserted hallway of the hospital toward the call room, my legs felt heavy, and my neck ached at the weight of all the reference books stuffed in my long white coat. I *longed* to sleep.

When I unlocked the door to the call room, the streetlights from the parking lot outside the window cast a dim fluorescent glow across the floor. I kicked off my shoes and tossed my pager on the table as I stood for a moment, quietly surveying the room. What a sad place. One little twin bed sat against stark white walls with an orange plastic chair in the corner and itchy industrial carpet underneath my feet. This sad little room where I always returned to rest after hours of work was a great companion to my life, actually. Pathetic.

I felt pathetic.

And *so very tired.*

Complete and utter exhaustion settled itself way down deep in my bones. I was physically tired from lack of sleep. And I was equally tired of all the sadness. My loneliness. The lost feeling. My pain.

I knew I should lie down. Rest. Sleep. I would be up again in less than two hours to begin my morning rounds. But suddenly, as I stood there so tired and so sad and so very alone, spontaneous sobs erupted from my lungs. I couldn't hold them back. I stumbled over to the bed as the loneliest possible pain wracked my body, and I fell to my knees on the floor.

I could not imagine living another day this way. I couldn't possibly imagine any more pain. I couldn't imagine walking even one more step of this ridiculously sad life alone. I was too weak to pick up my weapons or carry any shield. I needed change. I needed *help.* I needed God. And right there in that sad, pathetic little call room, I gave up.

I bawled.

Loud and long and wailing. I let it all come out. Everything. All the pain I'd been carrying. My sadness. The incredible loneliness gripping my heart.

And for several minutes, there were no words. Only wailing. Until my voice was hoarse and my whole body hiccupped and shook like a two-year-old having a temper tantrum.

Then I began to cry out.

"I can't. I can't. I can't I can't I can't. I can't do this. God, I can't."

This was my prayer.

I had prayed a million times before, of course. I had "handed it over" to a Higher Power as Al-Anon instructed me to do. But I had always taken it right back. Immediately.

This night was different.

I was done. Done. I was utterly broken. I knew our marriage was broken. My husband was broken. And I knew, way deep down inside, he was probably going to die. I couldn't help him. There was nothing I could do for my husband. I *could not* save him. He was going to die.

The pain from this realization was unbearable.

I can't.

But then, very quietly in the middle of all my crying and wailing and calling out in desperation, a brand-new thought crept in for the first time, *Maybe . . . maybe I could save me?*

And this was my breakdown moment.

My surrender.

My cold and broken hallelujah.

I reached my hands up over my head like a child reaching to be picked up, and from the bottom of the pit I'd been living in for years, I cried out, *Help! Heeeeelp!!! Oh please, won't you save me?? I'm down here!! HEEEEELP!!! Please. Please, God! Oh please, won't you help me?*

Then, from the rocky bottom of that pit on my knees, broken and sad and lonely and lost and so utterly and completely alone, I whispered this last desperate plea:

"I'm giving this to you. I'm giving this to you. I'm giving this to you."

I gave Him my husband. And our marriage. I gave Him our family. And my pathetic little life plan. I gave it *all* to Him. Everything. All of me. I prayed and pleaded.

I'm giving this to you.

Over and over and over and over.

This was the night I gave Him my life.

And nothing happened, it seemed. An hour or so later, I woke up, brushed my teeth, hoisted my heavy white coat off the back of that orange plastic chair and onto my shoulders, tucked my pager onto my scrub pants, and headed out for rounds with red puffy eyes—just a few more hours before I could go home.

I went back to work. And everything felt the same.

But then somehow, on a random Wednesday morning about six months later, one of my husband's mandatory drug screenings came back positive. And during what felt like the absolute end for my little family, as I watched my husband drive off for rehab for a second time, I felt a big, strong, comforting hand reach down and pluck me out of "the bottom."

The hand of *LOVE* pulled me right up out of that deep, dark, lonely pit.

He was there all along. I was never alone in my pain. He listened. God saved me.

He brought me *home*.

> I waited patiently for the LORD;
>   he turned to me and heard my cry.
> He lifted me out of the slimy pit,
>   out of the mud and the mire;
> he set my feet on a rock
>   and gave me a firm place to stand.
> He put a new song in my mouth,
>   a hymn of praise to our God.
> Many will see and fear the LORD
> and put their trust in him.
>
> Psalm 40:1–3

SIX

my unraveling

What screws us up most in life is the picture in our head of how it is supposed to be.

I stood in our bedroom doorway and stared, silently watching the two of them sleep. I tried to memorize the way my little boy's three-year-old arm wrapped under his daddy's shallow pick-marked cheeks and how the warm summer sunshine streamed through the lace curtains on our window, casting lacy shadows across the yellow quilt on our bed. My husband would leave for rehab that day.

And time had stopped completely.

My heart—my soul—felt empty as I just stood there. Watching. Staring. Holding the beautiful life I was *supposed* to be living like a fragile glass ball in my hands.

Even now, thirteen years later, when I close my eyes, I can put myself on the exact day, in the exact moments he left our house for a second stay in rehab. This stay would be followed by a six-month separation while he lived in an addiction three-quarter-way house. And I understand now, this was the day everything began to change.

An end.

And a beginning.

For some reason, the song "Chasing Cars" by Snow Patrol echoed in my ears. Because for years, I thought we could do it all. . . .

Everything. On our own.

Without anyone or anything.

And I know I've made it sound like *every* moment of our marriage was awful. And many were. But so many more were breathtakingly beautiful too. Like buying our first car and marveling at how fancy we were in our very own Nissan Sentra. Like signing the paperwork on our first little house and pinching ourselves because we were homeowners now. Like finding a stray kitty on the side of the road and welcoming it home. Like the holy moments of becoming a family together and the memory of staring through our tears into the face of a whole new little person, a piece of *us*. Like going to IHOP for pancakes at 3 a.m. on our first outing as a family of three. It was all so beautiful. We had a *beautiful* life. Not perfect in the slightest, but *ours*.

And this felt like the end.

In that heart-wrenching moment, *every* feeling inside me wanted to crawl into bed beside the two of them and pretend. Pretend this wasn't happening. Pretend this wasn't my life. Pretend I was actually living the glass-ball life. The perfect life I'd been chasing for so long.

Happily ever after.

I wanted to forget the entire world and lie there beside my husband, the only man I'd ever loved, with our little boy asleep between us and our baby napping in his crib in the nursery next door. I wanted to pretend we were all taking a nap on a Sunday afternoon. And we would wake up and go for a walk and push the double stroller to the park. Then we'd laugh and give our boys underdogs on the swings and spend time together as a family without a care in the world before we came home to make dinner. Together. I wanted to pretend drugs and alcohol didn't overshadow everything.

I wanted the glass-ball life. I wanted it *all*. I wanted so badly to pretend.

But I didn't.

This was the day I *stopped* pretending.

Brené Brown calls this *the unraveling*. She says the unraveling is "a time when you feel a desperate pull to live the life you want to live, not the one you're 'supposed' to live. The unraveling is a time when you are challenged by the universe to let go of who you think you are supposed to be and to embrace who you are."[1]

> "The unraveling is a time when you are challenged by the universe to let go of who you think you are supposed to be and to embrace who you are."

Who you actually are.

I wanted to pretend. But that day, in simultaneous acts of unparalleled courage and utter defeat, I opened my clenched fists. And released it. All.

I let go.

And the beautiful life that was *supposed* to be crashed to the wood floor and shattered into a hundred million pieces. I stood for just a moment with the soul-crushing agony of my empty hands. My heart stripped. Bare. With all the broken bits of life scattered at my feet.

I stood in my unraveling.

Then I dropped to my hands and knees and began sifting. I fumbled through the broken shards of my life looking for anything I *chose* to remain in a life I *wanted* to live.

I chose Jesus.
I chose Love.
I chose Mercy and Peace.
I chose Gentleness and Grace.
I chose Kindness and Patience.
I chose Faith.

Then I gently rose on shaky legs and tucked all those broken bits carefully into my pocket. And I began again. I lived. I prayed and worked and laughed and loved and left my hands open and free. Day after day after day I felt those loose pieces tumbling against one another in my pocket. Until years later, many years later, when one day I pulled those broken pieces from my pocket and noticed they'd been worn smooth. And beautiful. Just like sea glass.

Because when we let go, when we let ourselves unravel, a new feeling has room to emerge. And it's so unmistakable.

Joy.

SEVEN

sunset moments

It was the strangest feeling, the first time I ever said the truth about my husband's addiction and our failing marriage *out loud* somewhere other than within the safety of Al-Anon's walls. To a near stranger.

The week my husband left for rehab a second time, I missed two days of my monthlong orthopedics rotation at the hospital. On the first day, I didn't even attempt to go to work. I left the boys at their grandparents' house overnight and spent the day wallowing in the eerie silence of our quiet home and sobbing through that gut-wrenching loneliness. The second day, I attempted to go to work, but once I pulled my car into the parking lot, I couldn't seem to get my legs to move my body out of the car. They felt like lead weights. Unmovable. So I sat for nearly an hour alone in my car. Willing myself to walk into the hospital. But I just couldn't move. I was frozen to my seat.

By the third day, I knew going to work was inescapable. So I wore my very best dress. I fixed my hair and applied makeup and wore high-heeled sandals (how practical). And when I walked into the clinic, my attending physician looked a little miffed and asked, "Where have you been?"

Then, for the first time in what felt like my whole life, I told the truth. I didn't make excuses or feign illness or gloss over the gory details or apologize. I didn't pretend. I was *so done* pretending. I said, "Well, actually, my husband is in drug rehab for a second time, and I guess I'm really struggling with it. I needed a couple of days to myself."

His mouth fell open just a little bit.

And then this mid-forties, often mildly inappropriate, hot-headed orthopedic surgeon who was known to do post-op exams with a dip of chew in his mouth, said, "What?! My God! Mikala. *Look* at you. You're absolutely *beautiful*! And *smart*! You're *amazing*! You could have any man you want!! You should just leave him."

It wasn't the response I expected. It was probably a border-line inappropriate thing to say as his eyes looked me up and down in my dress. But it was exactly what I needed to hear. And for the first time in my entire life, I thought to myself, *I know*.

Because my whole life I'd been the model codependent. I nursed until I was three, slept on my parents' floor next to their bed until I was eight, dated essentially *one* boy who, to this day, remains the only person I've ever slept with, moved directly from my family's house to a sorority, and then directly into my first apartment as a newlywed to my high school sweetheart.

I didn't know how to exist on my own. I truly didn't think I could survive if I wasn't connected to another person for support. I convinced myself that once we were married, Dan and I should be like *one* person. I thought his troubles were my troubles. And his successes were my successes. And his life was my life.

I believed there was no one else in the entire world who would ever want to have me. After all, I basically grew up on Dan's arm. Who would I be if not *Mikala Albertson, Dan's wife*? He was supposed to be my happily ever after, right?

But I finally told the truth out loud that day, and after my attending's perfect response, my shoulders lightened a little bit. My head rose just a smidge higher. Suddenly, my heart wasn't beating quite so fast. And I kept thinking, *He's right. I KNOW!*

I finished out the day at work and drove to pick up the boys. I fixed us a picnic for dinner, then jogged with the double stroller around the path at our neighborhood park. We stopped near the playground and ate our sandwiches, then I pushed my little boys on the swings and gave them underdogs, and we laughed and laughed. Afterward, we went home for bath time and books before bed.

I prayed.

I got up and went to work. I bought groceries. I paid bills. I mowed the lawn. I got together with my girlfriends. I went to Al-Anon meetings. I stayed up late watching movies or reading or scrapbooking.

Every day, every moment, I did *just the next right thing*. And I noticed how the entire house and everyone in it breathed a sigh of relief. Because suddenly anxiety and fighting and sadness and arguing and monitoring and lying and anger and crying and sleeplessness and fear had walked right out the door.

I was living. Truly *living* all by myself.

My husband was away at drug rehab, and he wouldn't be returning for six months while he lived in a three-quarter-way house as part of his recovery. And I was still *alive*. Maybe truly alive for the first time in my entire life.

I *needed* that time. I needed to know I could survive. I needed to know I could thrive on my own. Somehow, during those months apart, I laid down any expectation of moving forward, and I lived every single moment in the here and now.

When I spent a long weekend visiting my husband in rehab a few weeks later, I noticed how his eyes weren't foggy like they used to be, and his skin had cleared. He'd gained a good ten pounds. He seemed gentler and happy and different and also *exactly* like the person I fell in love with.

How nice, I thought. And basically shrugged.

Because who knew how long it would last? Who knew what would happen next? *Who knew?* I couldn't worry about that anymore. I was too busy living.

This time, as I sat beside him in meetings and small groups, I looked around at all the people sitting there with us, and once again everyone else seemed to be really struggling too. Broken homes. Broken marriages. Bankruptcy. Chronic disease. Homelessness. Missing teeth. Jail time. IV drug use. Broken lives. And while the details varied, all of it sounded a lot like our problems. And I was pretty sure we were *exactly* the type of people who belonged there. Every day we sat together in this group of the loveliest, most broken, and breathtakingly beautiful people. Sharing our stories right out loud to the room. Using feeling words and crying or shouting out the real, actual, honest *truth*. I had never felt so much at home. And after every small group meeting, we offered each other hugs and support. Sometimes we held hands and prayed together. And we recited the Serenity Prayer about twenty times a day.

God, Grant me the Serenity to accept the things I cannot change, the Courage to change the things I can, and the Wisdom to know the difference.

I couldn't remember ever feeling more myself. And I decided I never wanted to pretend again.

One evening during my stay, Dan had permission to leave the rehab facility so we could celebrate our seventh wedding anniversary in a dingy little Mexican restaurant in downtown O'Neal, Nebraska. We sat down at a small table in the back on some mismatched chairs with ripped plastic coverings that scratched at my legs. My eyes darted from the vases of faded yellow flowers decorating each table to the straw sombreros and black-and-white pictures of the old downtown adorning the faux wood paneling on the walls. Internally, I sighed and imagined this must be the "for worse" part of our wedding vows. But then dinner began, and we laughed and talked and made sarcastic jokes and looked at one another in the eyes. *Oh, here he is!* I thought to myself as I tried to memorize the look of my husband's face and his bright, clear eyes. Gosh, I'd missed him. This was exactly the man I married.

But the next evening, I hugged him good-bye and went home. Because who knew how long it would last? Who knew what would happen next? It didn't matter so much to me anymore. I just wanted to keep on living.

On the drive home, God showed up right there in my car to love me through the sunset with oranges and pinks and yellows set above rolling green farms on a warm July night. I remember thinking, *I might have missed this lovely moment if I weren't taking this drive.* I realized in that beautiful moment, God shows up to shine His love down on me in the most unexpected places sometimes. Like there in the restaurant as I laughed and talked with the man I married. And here on this breathtaking drive.

I remember thinking, *This is a sunset moment.* Because even on the darkest and hardest and saddest of days, beauty appears. Often where I least expect it. And even if that beauty is only fleeting, like the sunset, it is my daily reminder of God's love.

Now I use the term *sunset moment* for all the fleeting moments of beauty in my life. Moments that sneak up out of nowhere and take my breath away. And although they never seem to last long enough, I can be sure that even as one passes, another will be on the horizon soon. No matter what happens, the sunset *will* come. And God will shine down in oranges and pinks and yellows as if to say, *Don't forget, sweetheart. I LOVE you. And I'm right here. I'm always right here.*

Once home, I interviewed for my first real job as a family practice doctor and negotiated working only three days a week because I knew I needed some time at home with my boys. I had missed far too much with them already during those long call nights of residency, and I longed for a chance to really breathe.

I chose the finishes and décor for a new house we were building—a house I could afford all on my own with my new part-time doctor's salary. And whenever I visited that house during the construction process, I pictured living there as a single mom with two little boys *or* as a family of four with certainly more babies to come. I walked room to room envisioning where we might put our couch. I imagined the long wooden farmhouse table I planned to buy one day and daydreamed about pancakes in the kitchen on Saturday mornings. And sometimes, as I walked room to room picturing my new life in this new place, I heard the faintest little whisper: *"You're going to be just fine."* Me . . . with my two boys. Together. Or me . . . with my husband and our beautiful family. Together. Either one of these scenarios seemed a very fine option.

I relaxed. I smiled. I read books. I sat doing nothing. I laughed with my boys. I sat in the pain whenever it threatened to overtake me and cried myself to sleep. I felt it *all*. I let go over and over again. And I trusted God.

With my life in pieces all around me, for the very first time I *lived.*

EIGHT

queen martyr

Al-Anon's first public service announcement used to say, "You can see what the drinking is doing to the alcoholic. But can you see what it is doing to you?"

The last thing I ever wanted in my whole life was to be a part of Al-Anon. *Sigh*. Poor me. Add it to the list of things in my life that weren't going according to my perfect master plan.

After my husband returned from rehab, the two of us started going regularly to AA and Al-Anon meetings after church on Sundays while the boys went to their grandparents for a couple of hours. Every week we pulled up to this old white house with a big wraparound porch and mature trees and flowers in the yard. We parked along the road and walked together along the cracked sidewalks. Sometimes we held sweaty hands to steady each other. And every week we were greeted outside by a gruff-looking group of men smoking and laughing and holding white Styrofoam cups of coffee in their hands. Week after week they waved and greeted us cheerily through a cloud of gray smoke. "Welcome. How you two doin' this morning?"

It took me a while to notice their sincere smiles.

We walked into that old, musty house to the sound of chatter and chairs scraping wood floors as the smell of stale coffee filled the air. Then we parted ways. Because the important, life-changing work we'd be doing there was very individual. My Al-Anon meetings took place up some creaky stairs in a bedroom-turned-meeting room while AA meetings raged on in the living room downstairs.

The first time I walked into an Al-Anon meeting, I wore my martyrdom like a giant puffy coat. I thought surely everyone felt sorry for me. I felt certain I had the saddest, most pathetic story there. And clearly, I had every reason to skulk around in my giant puffy-coat-of-pain. Hood pulled up tight over my head. Hands stuffed deep within my pockets. That way I wouldn't have to get too close to anyone. That way no one would really be able to reach me. That way I could sit in my hot and sweaty pity pot feeling sorry for myself. A walking puffy-coated tragedy.

But then, one meeting, it was my turn to speak. I trembled a little as I stood at the podium to introduce myself. I wiped my sweaty palms on my jeans and launched into all the awful details of my current situation. I expected everyone to gasp. I expected tears. I expected clicking tongues and shaking heads and clutched chests. But mostly everyone listened intently and offered knowing smiles. Their eyes looked at me with encouragement and love. Many nodded. *Nodded their heads!* But no one spoke. No one offered advice. No one fixed or compared or shamed or glossed over my painful truth. They just sat there. Silently. Quietly refusing to let me be a martyr. Bearing witness to my unique story.

It was so confusing.

And frankly, I was a little pissed.

I stood up there in my giant puffy martyr coat and started sweating with rage.

I wanted to shout . . .

Didn't you people hear what I just said? My husband is a DRUG ADDICT! This is happening in my house! With my HUSBAND! I have two little boys and I'm working my tail off at the hospital and my marriage is crumbling and we are drowning financially and my entire life is hanging by a thread. . . . Why are you all just sitting there with those contented smiles on your serene little faces? I DON'T WANT TO HEAR YOUR "ME TOOS!" You should all be as shocked and appalled by my life as I am!!

But they weren't. How infuriating!

I sat down with a huff. I wanted to cry. I wanted to run out of there and never come back. These people couldn't possibly understand. I needed shock and awe! I needed pity! I needed someone to be angry at alcohol and drugs and absolutely pissed at my husband right along with me. Why didn't any of these people seem *ANGRY*?

But they just . . . weren't.

For some reason, I kept coming back. Maybe it was because of all those sayings (which initially made me even angrier).

Keep it simple.
Easy does it.
First things first.
Just for today.
Let go and let God.
Blah, blah, blah.

But I did. I kept coming back. I showed up. Week after week after week. I begrudgingly read all the books and those cheesy daily devotionals. I prayed. I started listening. *Really* listening to the awful, terrible, tragic stories of the people sitting next to me. The truth-tellers. Those people with kind eyes and wide smiles who took turns sharing story after story from their own broken lives, even worse (so much worse) than my own.

Listening is so healing, isn't it?

I noticed how the people with the most painful stories sometimes had the most serene smiles on their faces and how they leapt to help the next person in line. I noticed how they smiled and hugged people and filled up the coffeepot and beelined over to welcome the newcomers and lent out books and looked me right in the eyes with the *best* listening faces. I longed to know their secret. I was tired of feeling so angry. *How Al-Anon Works for Families & Friends of Alcoholics* says,

> In Al-Anon, it is often said that we are only as sick as our secrets. A key to breaking the stranglehold that alcoholism has on our lives is to begin to open up and let those secrets out. Part of the isolation of this disease is the belief that we are unique, that no one has done or said or felt the terrible things that we have done, said, and felt, and that no one could possibly understand. Therefore, we hide the truth at all costs. Until we challenge this sense of uniqueness by sharing our thoughts with other people who have known the shame and isolation of alcoholism, we may never find out that it is not real. . . . We who live or have lived with alcoholism have a rare understanding of one another.[1]

So finally, one meeting, I took off my coat. I hung it on the rack and noticed the entire coat rack was full. Without my giant puffy coat, I could give better hugs. And my hands were free to grab the hand of the person sitting next to me as we said our closing prayer. Without my coat of armor, I felt totally and completely understood. And suddenly I wasn't feeling so alone here anymore. For the first time ever, I realized with absolute certainty *we are not supposed to live this life alone.* And I couldn't wait to help the next person in line. In Al-Anon—and everywhere. Before long, I found myself smiling at the newcomers too. And nodding my head. Listening. *Really* listening. And wondering how long she was going to wear her puffy martyr coat. Wasn't she hot?

Eventually I found myself smiling at those gruff-looking men in their cloud of smoke outside and offering a cheery "Good morning!" After a while, I found myself walking away from meetings and smiling contentedly for no reason at all. I'd even dare to say my face began looking a little peaceful. And serene.

I learned to *tell the truth* in Al-Anon.

I experienced the incredible healing power of *listening* in Al-Anon.

I felt *SEEN and HEARD* in Al-Anon.

And now, all these years later, a good story is still my favorite thing in the whole wide world. Painful and sad and hilarious and ironic and bittersweet and tragic and happy and exhilarating and heartbreaking and true. I love them *all*! LIFE happens in our stories.

And I am willing to bet you have your own story to tell too. Because now I know we *all* do. Every single one of us has a messy, hard, beautiful, life-changing story to tell.

So take off your coat. Stay awhile in this lovely place called life. Grab my hand. Look around. Breathe. I'll be here listening when you decide to share. I'll be nodding with encouragement and love. I'll give you my most sincere smile.

And I'll hold space for you.

You . . . and your beautiful story.

NINE

one little box

The first box on my stack was small. And somewhere along the way, I'd wrapped it in pretty pink paper and tied it up with a big, beautiful bow like one of those fake decorative packages at Christmas—hoping that if the covering was beautiful enough, no one would ever know what I kept hidden inside.

But one day in the middle of my struggling life, my Al-Anon sponsor sat across from me at a small table in the back of a coffee shop, and her friendly blue eyes waited patiently as we sipped from our mugs. My secrets hid in that pretty pink box between us on the table. Bright and shiny.

Step Four of the Al-Anon recovery program involves making a searching and fearless moral inventory of ourselves. And now this was my Step Five: "Admitted to God, to ourselves, and to another human being the exact nature of our wrongs."

Because before any healing can take place, we have to begin at the beginning, don't we? With the stories and events that shaped who we are and how we've been created. We have to uncover the narrative we've been telling ourselves. And once we begin to understand who we are, we can move toward who we want to *become*. The truth sets us free . . . to be set free.

My sponsor smiled, and the deep dimples situated in each cheek flashed their encouragement and love. She waited. And sipped. And smiled. And loved.

So I looked down at my hands, and I just began. I pulled off the pretty pink bow and peeled back the paper. I opened the lid to my first little box and pulled out a tiny scrap of paper from inside. It looked like it had been folded at least a hundred times, into a teeny little square. I hesitated a moment before I slowly unfolded the crinkled edges and read the words scrawled in my eight-year-old print: "There is something very wrong with you."

I looked up at my sponsor then, tears welling in my eyes.

And I told her everything.

He simply asked if I wanted to go for a walk.

I can't remember how old I was exactly. Four? I can't remember if I asked my mom. I don't remember all the details of that day; we just went off together. Alone.

He took my hand, and I remember so vividly the feeling of my little hand in his and the way my arm angled up to meet his as we set out for a walk together, away from where the rest of the family was laughing and playing cards at picnic tables on the long, wide porch. Along the way, we found a baby turtle. I squatted down and poked at it. I picked it up and watched its legs struggle to find ground. I was *so* excited to bring a new pet along as we continued walking. And we ended up alone in the fenced swimming area. Just he and I. And our turtle.

As I told this story to my sponsor, it felt like I was transported up and away from our table in that little coffee shop. And I found myself watching it all from across the pool.

He's holding her little four-year-old hand, and in her other hand she's carrying that tiny green box turtle. Her blond hair is wild and frizzy from a day of swimming and playing in the sun. She's wearing a little purple swimsuit with matching white-and-purple checked shorts, her flip-flops clicking along with every step as they walk into the pool area together.

My eyes remain fixed on her little frame. She's so small. So sweet. So innocent. And she's thrilled to have found that turtle to play with.

They find a place to sit in the shade along the chain-link fence as the leaves of the giant sycamore tree flicker shadows across the hot pavement. The air is thick and humid, and the pool glistens so inviting and blue just a few feet away.

She chatters excitedly about that turtle. And then . . .

His hand moves toward her, but she doesn't move away.

"Can I touch you there?"

And she doesn't reply. She's frozen now, and she immediately stops talking as she pretends to be engrossed in the turtle crawling back and forth along the cement. He silently slips his fingers up her shorts and into her swimsuit. And I know it hurts a little, but she doesn't flinch. She doesn't even look up.

I want to holler across the pool, "Honey, NO! It's okay to tell him NO! Get up! Tell him NO!! Run back to your mom!"

But I can't.

I watch helplessly. I can only watch in silence from my perch across the pool as my life changes forever, and my stomach tightens with this familiar pit. I watch as he takes her hand again and leads her to his cabin while the turtle slinks away into the tall grass next to the fence.

And I know what happens next. I know she'll lie there motionless on the bed. I know she'll keep her eyes fixed on that dirty old screen above the bed, watching more sycamore leaves flashing in the breeze outside. I know she'll get up with him then and slip her shorts back on over her little purple swimsuit without a word. When he's finished.

And she'll believe him when he says, "If you ever tell anyone, I'll tell them it was your idea."

I know she never, never tells.

He grabs her hand again, and they walk back up the grassy hill in the bright July sun to join the rest of the family where everyone is still laughing.

I want to follow the two of them. I want to run up behind them and grab her little hand out of his. I long to hug her and hold her tight until she feels safe. Then pull her out to arms' length and wrap my hands firmly around her shoulders and look her straight in those beautiful hazel-green eyes.

It was my first day, my very first moment, for pretending. A secret at four years old.

And I want to tell her, "Honey, no. This was not your idea. This was not your fault. You didn't do *anything* wrong. You are *lovely*. But this is not okay. Go tell your mom. I know that sounds hard. Tell her. It never has to happen again. You won't be in trouble. Just tell the truth. Don't be ashamed. Go *tell* someone."

But she doesn't.

She doesn't tell. She pretends nothing happened. She pretends to be exactly the same.

It was my first day, my very first moment, for pretending. A secret at four years old. This was the very first day of my secret.

And so it happened again. And again and again and again.

It happened at Christmas celebrations. And family dinners. And once while riding along in the car in the dark with my mother sitting in the passenger seat up front. And at my grandmother's house. And during those summer trips to the yearly family reunion.

The secret grew. And grew and grew and grew.

I was ashamed. I didn't even know what *ashamed* meant. I

just knew how it felt. It hurt sometimes when he touched me, and I quietly winced. That's how shame feels.

I showed a cousin what he did to me and asked, "Does he ever do that to you?"

No. I was alone. The only one. And neither of us told anyone. So it became an even *bigger* secret.

I was sick a lot at family gatherings. I didn't want to go and play. I didn't want to leave the safe chatter of the adults in the kitchen. I didn't want to be away from my mother's side. And it went on this way for a couple of years until we moved to another town four hours away, and suddenly those years of touching and poking and prodding were over.

But the secret? And the shame?

They followed. They followed me to the new town. They followed me for so much of my life.

They followed.

I believed I was different. Different from everyone else. Different from all the other little girls. I believed this had *never* possibly happened to another living soul. I somehow knew more about my body than the other girls. I knew what hurt. I knew what felt good. And I knew that even what felt good must be wrong because it felt *so* wrong and left that familiar pit in my stomach.

I knew about boys. At four or five or six years old, I knew about boys. And fingers and mouths and kissing and tongues on private parts. And shame.

At four or five or six years old, I knew all about shame.

When I finished talking, my sponsor waited only a moment or two. Then she reached across the table and grabbed both my hands. Her bright blue eyes pierced into mine as she said with sincerity, "Mikala. I am so sorry that happened to you. I am so sorry you've been carrying that for all these years. It wasn't your fault, you know. Honey. Do you hear me? That wasn't your fault."

I felt just like a little girl as the tears I'd been stifling my whole life began to fall and I nodded. "Oh, I know," I lied. Except, I didn't know. Not really. And it was such a relief to hear.

So, I told her more.

Only this time, I had a new abuser—my grandfather.

Every year, my grandparents came to stay for a week while my parents went out of town for a work conference. And one evening, while my grandma was puttering with dinner in the kitchen, my grandfather and I sat together on the couch watching *Wheel of Fortune*. Out of nowhere I felt his hand on my thigh. And then ever so slowly his fingers crept higher and higher up my leg. I have no idea why I wasn't wearing pants. But I wasn't. Just a blue T-shirt and my underwear.

I was eight.

Eight is the age for performing gymnastics across the living room floor. Eight is the age for Barbies and Cabbage Patch Kids and playing school with my dolls all lined up on my bedroom rug. Eight is the age of running around without clothes on sometimes. Eight is the age of trusting the grown-up people in my life who are supposed to love me and take care of me and keep me safe. And for me, eight was the age when the awful thing that always left a pit in my stomach happened again.

He touched. And fondled. Keeping his fingers *just* outside my underpants. And I pretended nothing was happening. I didn't flinch. I didn't move. I didn't say a word. I was frozen. Again. Then when my grandma called from the other room, I'm pretty sure we just got up and ate dinner. I pretended I was fine. I pretended nothing happened. I pretended to be exactly the same. I was *so good* at pretending. After dinner, we played Parcheesi and laughed and carried on as normal while I tried to push the whole thing right out of my mind. After all, his hand stayed *outside* my underpants.

But then the next day, as I sat on my bed playing with my Speak and Spell, it happened again.

My grandparents had a routine of lying down for a little nap after lunchtime, and I thought they were napping. They were *supposed* to be napping. My grandma was napping. But suddenly, with my grandma asleep in the other room, my grandfather appeared in the doorway of my bedroom.

He sat next to me on the bed, and for a few minutes I pretended he wasn't there. I mumbled a few things about the game I was playing on my Speak and Spell and showed him my words. Bee boo beep. Bee boo beep. Perfect score!

And within minutes . . . there was his hand. Again.

But this time he hoisted his body back until he was lying behind me on the bed where I sat perched on the edge. I could feel him push his body up against my back as he wrapped his arm tightly around my waist and pulled me close. Into him.

He clutched at me. Desperate and fast. And this time I knew my grandfather was dangerous. This time I *knew* . . . things were about to get scary. So without any more silence or pretending or ignoring, I pushed his hand away and jumped up from the bed and hollered, "NO!"

That was it.

Just NO.

Then I turned and ran out of the room and straight out of the house. I hopped on my rusty old banana-seat bike and rode around the neighborhood while my cheeks streaked with tears.

My mind raced.

What is wrong with me? Why does this keep happening to me? What did I do? What if my parents find out? Now my grandfather? Who's next? My dad would be crushed to know his father did this to me. I can NEVER let them know. I can NEVER let anyone know. There is something wrong with me. I need to figure out what is WRONG with me!

I'm not sure how long I was gone.

And when I returned, everything was back to normal. I didn't say a word to either of them. We carried on with special desserts and Parcheesi and card playing. But I had come to a few conclusions while I was away.

I would never tell anyone.

I would never be alone with my grandfather again.

I would pretend to be *exactly the same* (even if everything about my world was suddenly different).

At eight years old, in addition to Cabbage Patch Kids and soccer practices and Barbies and gymnastics across the living room floor, it was my job to protect my parents from knowing this information. It was my job to prevent my grandfather from sexually abusing me. It was my job to figure out *why* this kept happening to me. It was my job to assume all men were scary and I should avoid every single one. It was my job to pretend I was just like the other girls . . . when, in my mind, I knew without a doubt I was *nothing* like the other girls.

That was the day I pulled out a little scrap of notebook paper and wrote a note to myself in my very best eight-year-old print: "There is something very wrong with you." Then I folded it up at least a hundred times into a teeny tiny square and shoved it into a little box. Wrapped it in pretty pink paper. And tied it with a pretty pink bow. Pretending and people-pleasing became my weapon, and perfection became my shield. And every day I pulled on my armor and hoisted up my shield so no one would ever be able to hurt the broken little girl hidden inside carrying all her pain and shame.

But sitting across from my sponsor in the coffee shop that day while the painful truth and her unconditional love hung in the air between us, I realized something.

Sometimes a true warrior surrenders her weapons and lays

down her shield. Then, with hands open and free, she lifts her head and walks forward . . . straight into life's pain. Regardless of the outcome. Once on the other side, she lays flat on her back gasping for air on that battlefield. And waits. She lets God stitch her back together. Fresh. New. Stronger than before. She is restored with Truth and Love. Then she stands. She looks down for a moment at the dried blood crusted on her hands, then back at the battle she overcame.

Without secrets, there is no longer a need for weapons or shields. So that fierce little warrior is free to turn and smile as she lifts her face to the sun, whispering, *"What's next, God? I'm ready to carry on."*

TEN

brokenhearted

God approaches us in the disguise of other people.
—Glennon Doyle, *Carry On, Warrior*

I'm pretty sure there's a reason I began practicing medicine to heal the sick and broken at the very same time I myself was brokenhearted. God had a plan there, it seems. He uses our brokenness and brings beauty to our hard stories in order to transform our lives. And those early years of practicing medicine proved to be extremely healing—for my loneliness and for my broken heart and for *me*.

In the beginning, I wanted to be a doctor for selfish reasons, really. I wanted a challenge. I wanted a job that would be well-respected. I wanted to make good money. I wanted to begin my *perfect* life, right? So after receiving my undergraduate degree, I spent the first two years of medical school studying and memorizing and toiling away in the anatomy lab. Cramming for endless hours before exams. Stressing and not sleeping and treating what felt like a stomach ulcer with Tums. And I finished those first two years of medical school somewhere in the middle of the pack. I passed.

Then, during my third and fourth year of medical school and for three years of family practice residency after that, while my husband sank further into his addiction and our home life was hard, I began taking care of actual patients in the hospital. Real people. Other hurting human beings with stories so much harder than my own.

And it absolutely changed my life.

Who knew people could be so broken? Who knew *everyone* has a story to tell? A painful past? Or a current ongoing struggle? And who knew none of us are ever really alone in this life? Who knew we're actually all in this together? And really, who knew other people's stories could be hard, and so very heartachingly beautiful too?

Every day during those years, I heard story after story of life's bitterness, brokenness, and pain. All the intimate details. And I quickly realized what a privilege it was to be a part of it all. How amazing it was to help in any way possible and to love other hurting people however I could. Residency was the place I truly learned about *love*. I found myself absorbed in my patients' stories. And though the details varied, I could see myself in each one.

Writer and theologian Henri Nouwen says, "It is my growing conviction that my life belongs to others just as much as it belongs to myself and that what is experienced as most unique often proves to be most solidly embedded in the common condition of being human."[1]

Before sitting in those tiny, curtained hospital rooms listening to sick and hurting patients pour out their stories and share their ailments, I honestly never knew about the common condition of being human. I convinced myself I was the only one struggling. I became so caught up in my *own* pain that, somewhere along the way, I stopped really seeing other people. And I honestly felt so alone in this life. But then, as I worked hour after hour into the night, as I learned how to cure others of their ailments, as I practiced really listening and loving my patients, it turned out my patients actually began curing *me*.

Like one morning, a whole group of us "smart people" in long white coats filed into a patient's room on the ninth floor to find a woman sitting on her hospital bed alone. She looked up and listened in silence as the attending physician explained her MRI results. She had MS.

Multiple sclerosis.

In his thick foreign accent, the head neurologist went on to explain she'd likely be in the hospital another day or two on IV steroids and then discharged home, with plans for her to come back into the clinic for further work-up to determine whether she had relapsing-remitting or progressive MS, and which medications might be appropriate, and blah, blah, blah.

But I couldn't stop looking at her face. I couldn't stop staring at the complete and utter bewilderment in this woman's eyes. It was somewhere around 7 a.m. and she had no family or friends with her for support. She sat quietly in her hospital gown on the edge of her bed as this group of six or seven white-coated doctors in various levels of training gathered around, listening to someone deliver news that would change her entire life.

At the end of this long speech, the group of "smart people" waltzed out in one fell swoop. After all, we had a *long* list of patients to see with hours of work ahead of us. As we filed out, another resident in the group quietly said something to her about how one of us would be back later to discuss discharge planning.

But she just sat there.

Quiet.

Stunned.

Alone.

And as the group of "smart people" I was traveling with continued down the hall to the next room, I couldn't stop thinking about her face. And her scared, sad eyes. So I fell away from the group and circled back. I knocked lightly on her door and found her still sitting on the edge of her bed in the same position.

"Did you understand all of that? Do you want me to go over any of it again? Or maybe . . . do you just need some company?"

And she looked up at me then. Her dark brown eyes fixed with mine.

I noticed the rich caramel color of her skin, and the faint lines on her forehead and around her eyes from years of worry and laughter and *life*. She had pulled her hair up into a brightly colored scarf tied in a knot on the top of her head. And tears trickled slowly down her cheeks.

I sat next to her on the bed and took her hand in mine. Pressing her smooth, dry skin against my own, I noticed her nails were long and yellowed and weathered from time. And with our hands clasped together there on the edge of her bed, I did my best to re-explain what she'd just heard. I did my best to put a little sense into the diagnosis that had just changed everything about the life she'd been living. I did my best to make certain she no longer felt alone. Then I sat there quietly beside her for a long while. Waiting. Just being present. Squeezing her hand and loving her until she was ready to speak.

And finally, she hugged me. A desperate kind of hug. I will never forget it, because in that moment, I knew. *This is what I'm supposed to do.*

A few years later I started practicing in my own clinic, and one morning I met Missy. She was in her mid-fifties, and her autism meant she still lived in her parents' basement. For most of her adult life she refused to leave the house to go anywhere other than the bar because she lived to play Keno and drink beer. Her parents brought her to my office for the first time in a last-ditch effort to do *something* because their daughter had lost at least fifty pounds and stopped eating and rarely wanted to do anything around the house because she was so tired. I watched my new patient walk in from the waiting room and step on the scale as the nurse checked her in, and thought, *I wonder where her cancer is?* I had never been so sure of a diagnosis at first glance.

It turned out her cancer was everywhere.

I convinced Missy that she needed to go to the hospital for further tests and IV fluids because she was severely dehydrated. And every morning during rounds, I spent an extra thirty minutes in her hospital room. Just chatting. When I walked in with the chart she always said, "What's up, giiiiirl?"

We didn't talk much about cancer. We never talked about medications or the fact that her oncologist decided there was nothing to help the cancer filling every crevice of her body. We never talked about hospice or how much time she had left. We just talked. And enjoyed one another's company.

When she went home on hospice, her parents initially refused to let Missy go to the bar. Her mother called me in a panic because her daughter was throwing tantrum after tantrum. And I spoke honestly with her mother. "What's it going to hurt, really? If she can still muster the energy, why not let her go? What if you dropped her off for an hour? What if you spoke with the bartender about keeping an eye on her? And limited her to a beer or two? They know her so well there already. And it's her very favorite thing."

I knew her time was limited.

So they took her a few more times. Dropped her off for an hour. Let her drink a beer or two and play Keno.

Eventually she was too weak to even *want* to go to the bar. Missy died a few weeks later. Her parents told me she died peacefully at home under hospice care.

A month or so later I found a gigantic dusty box on my office desk. My nurses had absolutely no information about it, and initially I was a little worried. *Could it be a bomb? Who is this from? Is something living inside it?*

But I worked up the courage, and I opened this huge box to find it was filled with model car sets for my boys. Missy's family had always assembled model cars together while she was growing up, and they knew I had a whole herd of little boys. Her parents figured my boys would love it—and they were right! What a perfect thank-you gift from Missy and her family.

The truth is, I am not the smartest of the smart people. I am not the most highly trained. I don't have awards or accolades. I'm not a specialist at anything. And most of the time, I worry to the depths of my soul that I'll miss something one day or make a bad decision.

But I am good at *people*. I am good at seeing people. I am good at loving people.

It is my *job* to love people.

This is medicine to me. It's love. And service to others. It's connection. And sharing. It's listening and learning about and helping another human being. And finding the beauty in another's story—a fellow child of God.

What a *gift* I've been given to have this privilege, to be entrusted with other people's stories. Really. It brings tears to my eyes. Because truly, in so many ways during that difficult, broken time in my life, practicing medicine was so healing . . . for *me*.

In this life, we heal each other.

ELEVEN

i want ordinary

What if everything is available to us right here in the middle of ordinary, regular life?

—Jen Hatmaker, *Of Mess and Moxie*

Shortly before my husband left for rehab and my perfect life-plan imploded, a mom and her children came to see me in the clinic for well-child physicals for each of her five kids. She was probably eight or ten years older than I, and after just a few minutes of conversation with her, I made my initial conclusion: She was absolutely amazing. And calm. And happy. She wore jeans and a T-shirt with flip-flops, and her hair was pulled back into a messy ponytail. Her children had clearly dressed themselves in clothing passed down from kid to kid to kid. She stayed home with her big brood and homeschooled them all and seemed so *content* with her life's circumstances.

She wasn't fancy or special or overachieving. She was quiet and ordinary and unassuming. She laughed easily and smiled often. I noticed how she spoke gently to each of her children.

I noticed how patient she seemed, despite the inevitable chaos of an exam room packed with five children. I noticed how she hugged them close or tousled their hair and smiled with pride as they took turns answering my questions. And more than anything else, I noticed *she so obviously loved her life.*

I want an ordinary life in an ordinary house on an ordinary street.

Together we reviewed all the children's immunization records. I asked all the necessary questions about medical history and reviewed everyone's milestones. My nurse tested their eyes against the eye chart, and I listened to their little lungs and checked their backs for scoliosis. I filled out the required paperwork for her son's Boy Scout camp later that summer.

We chatted freely as I worked, and I asked, "You guys have anything special planned this summer? Are you taking any trips?"

To which she smiled and replied, "Oh no. Nothing special. With me staying home, money is tight. We don't have any big, fancy trips scheduled. But my husband has a little camping weekend planned for us in August."

I remember wishing I could somehow spend more time with this amazing woman and her beautiful family. She seemed a lot more like a friend I might enjoy going out to lunch with rather than a patient. She smiled and thanked me as they left the clinic, and I walked quietly into my office and sat down. I took it all in, and I fought back tears as I realized with conviction, *I want that.*

I want *ordinary.*

I want an ordinary life in an ordinary house on an ordinary street.

I want a house full of kids and noise and fun so I can cook them giant pots of spaghetti and dance in the kitchen and holler at them to stop teasing each other and hang up their bags and put away their shoes and get started on homework already.

I want a herd of kids dressed in hand-me-down clothes passed from kid to kid to kid, and Saturday morning soccer games or weekend camping trips, and days spent at home taking care of all of them in my jeans and a T-shirt with flip-flops.

I want a sober husband who will walk in from work every evening to children's voices yelling, "Daddy's home!" And while I stand at the stove stirring that giant pot of spaghetti for dinner, he'll walk over behind me and wrap his arms around my waist and kiss my neck and ask me about my day.

Suddenly, in that moment, sitting in my office with tears streaming down my cheeks, my grand plan for a perfect life—the master plan I'd been striving for my entire life—seemed so silly. So impossible. So shallow. So stupid.

I'd been working toward the wrong goal all this time. I was killing myself chasing perfection, but really?

I just wanted ordinary.

No more yelling or fighting or silent treatments. No more chasing or performing or striving. No more uncertainty around my husband and his addiction. No more wondering if he would be okay—if *we* would be okay. No more listening to the world's opinions or other people's expectations about who I should be or what I should do or exactly what our family should look like. No more stewing over whether this "perfect" life-plan would ever become a reality.

I was worn out. Tired. Spread too thin. Absolutely exhausted. And utterly defeated.

And the truth was, I didn't want perfect—I wanted *ordinary*.

Jen Hatmaker says this about finding the extraordinary in a good, hard, ordinary life:

We have been warned that *ordinary* is less than, a sign of inferiority, an indicator that so much more awaits if we could just get the mix right. But the truth is, most of life *is* pretty ordinary, so it is precisely inside the ordinary elements, the same ones found the world over—career, parenting, change, marriage, community, suffering, the rhythms of faith, disappointment, being a good neighbor, being a good human—that an extraordinary life exists.[1]

For so many years—for most of my life, really—I had never given myself the room or the space or the grace to *exhale.* I just kept taking in giant gulps of air and trying to hold it all in for fear of losing. Losing something I wasn't even sure of. Inhaling and inhaling and inhaling until my lungs stretched and burned and seared with pain. Until my brain screamed for me to exhale, and my whole body felt as though I might explode.

Until my life actually exploded.

But that day in clinic, with a broken heart from all the pain of my broken life at home, I sat with this calm, quiet, ordinary woman. And I watched her breathing in and out. In and out. I noticed her laughing and talking and loving on her children.

I gaped at her easy, breezy way.

I marveled at her contentment.

And in that moment, the most beautiful, peaceful truth occurred to me: We don't have to keep inhaling and inhaling and inhaling every drop of air until we can't fully breathe.

More and more and more air isn't actually *better.*

We can exhale.

Then on the next breath in, we can let our chests rise just enough for a refreshing breath of air to rush in and fill every space. And at the natural pause of a normal breath, all that fresh oxygen can fill our blood and rush off to every cell in our bodies to offer sweet release.

Then we can exhale again.

We can breathe out all the used-up air, and our chests can fall without worry because the next refreshing breath is right there. Already on its way in. Over and over and over.

We don't have to struggle and gasp and strive. We can just inhale and exhale. In and out. In and out. We can let go. We can live this ordinary little life exactly as God has planned.

We can breathe.

LIFE happens in the ordinary. And I just want *ordinary*.

TWELVE

jesus, be near

Not all of us can do great things. But we can do small things
with great love.

—Mother Teresa

As a young resident, I'd only been involved in a handful of code
situations, and usually I found myself being pushed to a back
corner of the room where I could absorb the hustle and bustle
and chaos from afar.

One person "runs" the code. Another takes charge of the
airway by applying a mask and delivering oxygen into the
lungs with every squeeze of the attached bag. And yet another
administers chest compressions. One nurse draws blood for
laboratory work while another pulls out the medication cart
already prepared for emergency situations with medications
like atropine and epinephrine. Then out comes the ECG to get
a heart tracing, and the paddles for shocking, if needed.

Everyone has a job to do, and the whole situation feels like
the workings of a well-oiled machine while a human life hangs

in the balance underneath. I never, ever lost my fear and amazement and bewilderment and awe in code situations, even if I was typically only peripherally involved.

Then one shift, around 3 a.m. while on call, I walked with two other residents to take a patient down for an MRI. I didn't know this patient well at all. I didn't know her name. I'd never spoken with her while she'd been coherent. I didn't know the details of her situation. But she was very sick, and the team needed a few extra hands for transport, so I walked along beside.

On our way back upstairs after the patient's study was complete, we huffed our way up a very long basement hallway and made small talk, all secretly hoping to head to our call rooms for a quick nap once she was settled back in her room. Suddenly, the patient vomited, and likely aspirated. And then coded right there in the hallway.

No pulse.

One resident immediately jumped up on the bed to start compressions while I helped the other resident finagle that bed back down the hall toward MRI as fast as humanly possible so we could push the button to call a formal code and get a team to come rushing with help.

And this time, instead of being shoved to the back of the room amid the chaos, I was the person monitoring her pulse until she was hooked up to the machines. Feeling for every compression of her chest to leave an impact on my fingers resting firmly on her wrist. Then straining at every pause to feel for an independent beat. I had a very small but important job right in the center of it all.

And as I sat there feeling beat after beat bump my fingers with every thrust, while everyone else bustled and hollered and buzzed around me, I thought, *I wonder where this woman is right now? I wonder if it's like the movies and she's floating somewhere above, just watching?*

I sure hoped not. I hoped the last image she saw was not of her vomit-covered, bulging, naked, jaundiced body being poked and prodded and pushed all alone in a room of strangers.

And maybe I was a little emotional from all the sleep deprivation, but suddenly another thought swept into my brain. *This woman was once a child. And I bet she LOVED the swings.*

Dear God, are you there?? Dear God, I hope right now she's on the swings.

And all I could do was pray.

Jesus, be near. Jesus, we need you. Jesus, she needs you. I prayed and prayed with every pulse against my fingers. *Jesus, be near. Jesus, be near. Jesus, be near.*

It occurred to me again that I didn't know her name. I didn't know whether she was married or had children. I had no idea where she was from or what she did for a living. I didn't know whether she was active in church or if she had been a member of the PTA. I mean, did she prepare home-cooked meals for her family every night? Who knew?

But I did know without a doubt as I held on to her wrist in those final minutes, this woman was a child of God.

And I couldn't help imagining her as a little girl on the swings. Smiling and laughing. Pumping her legs higher and higher until her toes brushed the tree branches above. Hair flying out behind, then swishing across her face on the downswing. Eyes closed and turned toward the glowing yellow light of the sun. Warm and bright. Bathed in the light.

Pure heaven.

And then I imagined Jesus standing alongside. Watching. Taking in the sight of His beautiful child happily swinging with glee. Back and forth. Back and forth. Loving her so fully and completely. And smiling a wide smile. So absolutely delighted by the joy on her face. Just waiting. And watching.

He didn't pull out a clipboard and holler questions like,

"Where did you go to church? Did you ever have the priest over for dinner? What about the annual fundraiser at school? Did you volunteer? Or donate? Were you active enough in your community? What was your yearly income? And where exactly did you store all your treasures? Honey, you look so happy right now, but tell me . . . in this life, were you GOOD enough???"

Nope. None of that.

He just smiled.

Pure love.

Then I imagined Him calling to her as she opened her eyes. A brilliant smile spreading across her face and lighting up her soul. I imagined she slowed the swing a little then as she stopped pumping, and she dragged her feet along the grass as He called out, "Are you ready?"

"Yes!!!" she replied as she vaulted out of the slowing swing and landed softly on the ground. She looked up at Him and smiled from her perch there on the warm, lush grass. Then she stood. So completely unafraid as He held out His hand. He'd been waiting for her . . . and she had known Him all along.

I imagined she took His hand confidently and walked beside Him as they went away together without ever looking back. I could see it all through the hustle and bustle and beeping and orders ringing out in the hospital room.

Jesus, be near. Jesus, be near. Jesus, be near.

And when someone eventually called the code and announced this beautiful child of God's time of death . . . I watched the two of them, this little girl and Jesus, walking hand in hand into that glowing yellow light.

Only love.

THIRTEEN

tell the truth

What kills a soul? Exhaustion, secret keeping, image management.

And what brings a soul back from the dead? Honesty, connection, grace.

—Shauna Niequist, *Present Over Perfect*

My whole life I was afraid to tell the truth.

Sure, I could tell the truth about little things, mostly. But I'm talking about the *big* things. I was afraid to tell the truth about the big things. Things like my failures and flaws. Things like my struggles and insecurities. The honest truth about my *real* self. About *me*. I thought if I told the truth, if I actually said it out loud, it might make me unlovable. Unworthy.

I was always so afraid.

I mean, why in the world would anyone want to share their awful, terrible truth? Isn't that scary? Isn't that just too big a risk? People don't love other people who struggle. People who stumble. People who fail. Do they? It always felt easier to just *pretend*.

But luckily, I had a pretty big stumble that showed me otherwise. Luckily, the near total destruction of my marriage and family and "perfect" life showed me I don't have to pretend. I can tell the truth. I can be me. My truth is beautiful! And I can pull my beautiful truth out of the box and give that gift to others because then maybe they can be brave enough to tell their beautiful truth too.

And that's just what happened when Joshua came into my office. His regular doctor's schedule was full for the day, so he booked an appointment with whoever was first available and came to see me instead. He wanted to get something for his anxiety, he said. It was just getting to be too much, he said. He was having trouble sleeping and it was affecting him at work, and he was feeling weird and uncomfortable when he was out with his friends, and he hated going into the store alone. He just needed something. A medication. Anything. He needed something to fix all this anxiety and stress, he said.

I listened intently, but I couldn't stop looking at his face. I couldn't help noticing that stale smell of alcohol and poison oozing from his pores and filling the room. I couldn't help but notice the fidgeting and restlessness and darting eyes and vacant stares.

And, as I would with any new patient, I asked him lots of questions about his history. What illnesses tended to run in the family? Who did he live with? Where did he work? Was he a smoker?

He seemed a little quiet about that one. He brushed past it. Yes, he drank every day, but it wasn't a problem. Well, not a big problem, anyway. It wasn't like he was an alcoholic or anything. . . .

So I waited.

I asked him a few more questions. Had he ever been in trouble with the law because of alcohol? Was it affecting his family? Or his job? Had he ever tried to cut back? Did he ever use alcohol to treat his anxiety? Did it help? Or make his anxiety worse?

Then I waited some more. I waited long enough to make him slightly uncomfortable. Long enough that, finally, he started talking.

And I listened. It turned out, alcohol *had* been a problem. A pretty big one, actually. He'd had one DUI. His wife had moved out, and she wasn't allowing their children to spend weekends with him anymore. He lost his previous job when he was found drunk at work, and he was currently working for his brother's business while living short-term with a friend. He felt as though if he didn't pull it together soon, his friends and family might give up on him completely. He'd had so many tries. And just that morning, his mother had come to visit. She sat across from him with concern in her eyes. Was he okay? Really??

And that's why he made the appointment. He couldn't wait until the next week when his primary doctor was available. It *had* to be today. He had to do something. He just couldn't go on another day like this.

Suddenly, I felt myself telling him everything. My husband's story. Our story. The *real* story. Before I knew it, the whole truth came out as I said something like this:

"Listen. I want you to know my husband is an alcoholic and drug addict. He was actively using for *years*. Seven years, in fact. He went to rehab twice. I honestly didn't think he would ever get better. I thought we were over. We have two little boys, and I was pretty sure I would be raising them all alone. He had criminal charges because of his addiction. He almost lost his job over it. He had so many chances. And we are still floundering in debt. He remains on probation at the hospital where he works and will be required to attend regular AA meetings and get random drug testing for the next five years. Before he went to treatment this last time, I was convinced, *convinced* that he was going to die. And I'm telling you all of this because I want you to know you *can* get better. You *can* stop drinking. You *can* get help. I promise, there is another way. There is a way out of all of this. It won't be easy by a long shot, but you can do it. *YOU CAN.*"

As I talked, I saw a few slow tears trickle down his cheeks. He watched my face with full attention. He seemed riveted by this truth. And I couldn't help noticing how his shoulders loosened just a little bit. How his face relaxed. How his hands stopped fidgeting. Maybe it was the first time he'd ever heard a *real truth* uttered out loud by a stranger. Maybe my truth made him feel a little less alone and afraid because, by the time I was done telling my story, he had broken into sobs.

Maybe my truth made him feel a little less alone and afraid.

Then his eyes met mine. "Well, what do I do next?" he wanted to know.

I told him I could call for a bed in a rehab facility for him that very day. We could call his friend who could pack up a few things and give him a ride. He could go right now. We could do something about it *right now*.

He worried about his job, of course. What would he tell his brother? What about work? Wouldn't his family be disappointed? And what would his friends say? And his co-workers? His mom? And what about insurance? And bills? What about all the things that needed to be taken care of while he was away?

I told him I understood his concerns, but wasn't this really a matter of life and death? Wouldn't his family and friends only want him to get well? And wouldn't they be able to help while he was away? And wouldn't most of it still be waiting for him when he got back? And if not, couldn't he just . . . begin again?

He agreed.

He sat in my exam room for at least an hour while I squared away the details before his friend came to give him a ride to the inpatient treatment facility. My other patients had to wait a little longer that day, of course. But today, for Joshua, this really was a matter of life and death.

A few weeks later, I drove to that same rehab facility with my husband to celebrate his one-year clean and sober anniversary, and to pick up his Sober Cup. During their thirty-day stay in rehab, the patients paint and decorate a cup with words or sayings or drawings or colors. Then, upon discharge from the facility, they hang their cups on hooks along the wall where they'll be displayed until the following year. If they've remained clean and sober for one full year, they can return to collect their cup and see all their counselors and say a few words to the current inpatient addicts. The first time my husband went away, we didn't go to collect his cup. He didn't make it anywhere near one year clean and sober. But this time, we left our little boys with their grandparents for the afternoon and made the four-hour drive.

This time was different.

I stood there next to my husband as he told his story and collected his cup. I said a few words myself and picked up the little scrapbook of quotes and Scripture I'd made and hung next to his cup the year before. And in the middle of it all, I felt a pair of incredulous eyes resting on me.

Joshua.

He was still undergoing treatment at the inpatient facility. He was just a few days from discharge. And on this day, his face was clear, his eyes were bright, and he was wearing the world's widest smile.

Afterward, as my husband chatted with a few counselors out front, I heard "Hey! Dr. Albertson!" from across the parking lot. I turned and saw Joshua all but running toward me. And there in the middle of the parking lot, he pulled me into a giant embrace, and our bodies pressed together in the most human way. Then this grown man's body shook as he sobbed against me and whispered, "Thank you. Thank you. Oh, thank you," into my ear over and over.

I love to tell the truth. I love to say things to make people feel hopeful about themselves and this life and God. Because the truth does that . . . it gives us *hope*.

FOURTEEN

for her

When people get sick, and suddenly doctor appointments and medications and endless bloodwork and dialysis or chemotherapy begin to dominate their days, what they tend to miss most is the *ordinary*. For a mom, this usually means grocery shopping or family dinners or late-night feedings or driving kids around to basketball games or soaking pudgy little bodies in the tub before bed.

I'm guessing that's how it felt for Kindra.

I bet she *longed* to have an ordinary day.

I met Kindra in the first year of my medical career after finishing residency. And honestly, she always made me feel a little inadequate. You see, during my medical training, I was part of a team. A whole team of doctors and nurses and nutritionists and social workers and pharmacists. And there were always one or two attending physicians in each rotation who were in charge of it all. The attending physician was an easy person to turn to with any of my questions. If I wasn't sure, I could ask the attending. And even when I knew the answer, even when I knew what to do, having a wiser, older, more experienced doctor looking over my shoulder gave me comfort.

So when I started out in my own clinic practicing all on my own, I was often terrified. Even after four years of undergraduate learning and four years of medical school and three years of residency training to become a family practice doctor, oftentimes I still felt unsure. I'd been in school for what felt like forever, but that still didn't make me feel like I should be in charge of people's hearts and lungs and blood sugar levels and thyroids and depressions and *lives*. I mean, what if I missed something? What if I didn't know what to do? What if I inadvertently hurt someone? *What if???*

Kindra was just like me—a mom. And in the end, she helped me waaaaay more than I ever helped her.

Every morning on my way to work I fervently prayed. *God, let my hands be your hands. Let my work be your will. Be with me. Help me. Bring the people I'm meant to love and serve today. And show me how to take care of them.* It was definitely more comforting to know I had Him on my side.

Then one day He sent me Kindra.

And I don't think the medical jargon really matters much in Kindra's story. The medical jargon could fill an entire book. It was so complex that a team of cardiologists and nephrologists and endocrinologists and infectious disease specialists and rheumatologists and ICU intensivists couldn't figure it all out, so I'm not going to get into that part.

What I do think matters about Kindra's story boils down to a couple of things: She was just like me—a mom. And in the end, she helped me waaaaay more than I ever helped her.

She came into my office as a young mom in her early thirties. And I bet the night before her appointment she'd been up with her two-month-old baby to feed him at least two or three times. I bet that morning before she dropped him at the sitter's, she nursed him again and patted his little back to burp him and kissed his temple and breathed in his soft, sweet scent.

I bet she hoped to be home before he needed to eat again, but I'm sure she left a bottle of pumped breastmilk in his stocked diaper bag just in case. I'm guessing she wanted to catch a nap in the afternoon while he was napping because, after all, she hadn't been feeling well for a while. And maybe she even had plans for what she would make for dinner that evening.

But I bet she never imagined that when I saw her in my office, her blood pressure would be quite so high. Dangerously high. Or her oxygen saturation would be below the normal limit as she huffed and puffed to tell me all her symptoms. And I guarantee she never imagined her ECG would be abnormal or that I would insist she head over to the hospital to be admitted immediately even though she protested because she didn't want to leave her little boy for even a minute longer.

I bet she never in a million years would have guessed that during the echocardiogram I ordered upon admission, she would acutely decompensate and need resuscitation, necessitating a several-week stay in the Intensive Care Unit.

(This is where all the medical jargon comes in. You know, the team after team of specialists for just about every organ system. And so many tests and blood draws and IVs and medications and CT scans and echocardiograms and dialysis and evaluations by just about everyone any of us doctors could think of.)

The cardiologist on her team told me on the first night of her hospital stay, "You know, if you'd sent her home from your office, she probably would've died." And I remember how I thought selfishly and proudly for just one teeny little moment, *Wow. I saved someone's life!*

But really it was only the beginning for Kindra. The beginning of month after month after month of doctors' visits and medications and three-times-a-week dialysis and follow-up testing. The whole works. She always came to see me in my family practice office with her curly-headed baby boy in tow. And honestly, I always felt completely inadequate. I so badly wanted to help. I wanted to *fix* her. I wished I could fix all of this. But there was very little I could do, the specialists ran the show. And mostly I was along for moral support. I helped make sure her stools stayed regular and monitored her erratic blood pressures and made sure her mood held up okay under all the stress. And I always, always remembered to ogle her beautiful baby boy. Somehow, he managed to continue growing through it all, as babies tend to do.

We celebrated when her kidneys improved and she stopped dialysis. We rejoiced when she managed to taper down to one daily blood pressure medication. I was so relieved to know she was improving. She was healing! And all of us were completely overjoyed.

It was just a month or so later that I got the call from a neighboring hospital.

Kindra had a stroke. A huge, dual-hemisphere hemorrhagic stroke. A completely life-altering, never-going-to-walk-or-talk-again stroke. A this-is-the-beginning-of-a-very-long-and-painful-end stroke.

I walked directly into my office that day and closed the door and put my head down on my desk and sobbed. Because I knew what this meant. I *knew*. That night after clinic, I picked my boys up from their grandparents' house and drove home. I put a pot of water on the stove and made pasta while my two little boys played and whined and laughed and argued and bickered and chased around my feet. The noise level after a long day at work was always an adjustment. But this time, instead of feeling overwhelmed as I stirred that giant pot with a wooden spoon, this little thought formed in my mind.

Kindra will NEVER get to do this. She'll never stand at the stove making dinner for her family while her children run and play and bicker and whine at her feet. She will never take her spaghetti-covered children up to the bath, then read them bedtime books before she tucks them into bed. She will NEVER again smell the top of her baby boy's head while she plants a kiss near his temple. Savoring that sweet, sweet smell created by God just for moms as she whispers, "I love you so much, sweetheart." NEVER.

I felt like I had failed. I wanted so badly to see her get better. But instead, over the next few years, I would watch her slowly deteriorate. After the stroke, she came into my office in a wheelchair, limbs now twisted with spasticity and nearly totally paralyzed except for her right thumb, which could give a thumbs-up. Head wrenched with such terrible and painful torticollis that her left cheek rested on her chest. And still with her curly-headed baby in tow, now toddling and climbing around on her wheelchair.

It was devastating to see.

And nothing was quite so difficult to watch as her spouse desperately trying to help her through it all. I watched him care for her with love and tenacity. Studying. Reading. Searching for specialists. Grasping for ways to alleviate her terrible neck pain. Researching anything and everything to help her improve. He cared for her all on his own, twenty-four hours a day, while also raising their toddler.

I watched him age at least ten years in just two. And I will never forget the look of defeat and sadness mixed with relief in his eyes when I told him something like, "It's okay, you know. It's okay to let go. To ask for help. To put her in a home where she can have twenty-four-hour care. You've done everything you could possibly do. It's okay. Really."

Years later, after Kindra spent some time in that long-term care facility, after my husband became clean and sober, after we moved our family to Utah and I became a mostly stay-at-home-mom, after *all* of it, I heard that Kindra had passed away. And all I could think was . . . *no more pain.*

A few years ago, I looked up her former spouse on Facebook. I wanted to know how he and their curly-headed baby boy were doing. And when the page popped open on my screen, there was their now eight-year-old boy with a wide smile, so proud at the fish dangling from his line. I audibly gasped and clapped my hand over my mouth, then said aloud to my living room, "Oh my God. Kindra! Your boy! He's beautiful!!" as my eyes filled with tears. And I probably shouldn't have, but I sent a little message to her spouse, saying I was thinking of them and hoping they were both doing well.

The truth is, I think of Kindra often. At dinnertime, while my family gives their high/low of the day. Every time I came home from the hospital with a new baby. Whenever I kiss the tops of little boys' heads on their first day of school. Special holidays. Or birthdays as we all sing "Happy Birthday" around our worn kitchen table. Random Tuesday afternoons pushing my kids on the swings. Nights of frustration trying to get everyone to just go to bed already.

Kindra's name slips into my brain right in the middle of an ordinary moment, and I remember. Kindra won't ever be able to do this. She'll never make a meal plan for the week, then traverse the aisles at the grocery store, lug all the bags to the car, and eventually pack it all onto the pantry shelves at home. She'll never move loads of superhero undies and stray socks and smelly basketball jerseys from the washer to the dryer to the ever-growing pile waiting to be folded. She'll never wait in the car pickup line and smile as kids run from school and little arms throw open the door, and she'll never exclaim, "Hey! How was your day?" as they climb in. She'll never stand cooking a giant pot of dinner at the stove while listening to every "Hey mom, guess what?" or overseeing first-grade math homework. She'll never drive kids back and forth to basketball or soccer practice or cheer from the stands for her boy on Saturday. She'll never have another bedtime with baths and that sweet-smelling baby lotion and books and snuggling next to her boy as she inhales the sweet scent all his own. Her life was cut short so unexpectedly. So abruptly. And she'll never have another lovely, messy, hard, wonderful, absolutely *ordinary* day.

She will never get that chance.

Sometimes right in the middle of my own ordinary life, the thought of her reminds me to savor every moment. To be present and soak it in . . . even the hard, messy, mundane parts. She reminds me to notice and breathe and listen and touch and taste *all* of it. This life. She reminds me to really *live* it. She reminds me *life* happens in the ordinary. What a gift.

Kindra was just like me—a mom. And she still helps me waaaaay more than I ever helped her.

Now she is gone.

And I am healing.

FIFTEEN

making amends

I spent years wanting it to be *his* fault. I wanted everything wrong with our marriage and him and our family and my life and me to be all his fault. I mean, certainly that was it. Right?

Why didn't he just stop drinking? Stop using drugs? Stop reaching out to whichever losers were selling him pills (and pot and powders and, well, you get the point)? Stop spending all the money we didn't have to get his next quick fix? Why?? And how, exactly, could he look me straight in the eyes or hug and kiss our little boys, then go and use drugs? Again? Didn't he understand the incredible pain he was causing? Didn't he realize the destruction he was bringing to our lives? His own? Our boys'? Mine? How could he continue to lie? How??

For years, I believed he was ruining everything. Alcohol and drugs were ruining *everything*. And for some reason, again and again, I believed he *chose* to use.

In the beginning, I decided it was my job to make it all better. My job to fix this problem. To fix him. And us. So I monitored everything. I watched. I counted. I complained. I cried. I lectured. I threatened. I yelled. It all became my obsession. His addiction was *my obsession.*

And I'm not sure how helpful it was to let him know that in a bottle of sixty pills (which weren't prescribed for him in the first place), taking ten or twelve or fifteen is too many. Waaaaay too many.

"YOU TOOK FIFTEEN TODAY!! I know, because I counted. I looked everywhere and found your hidden stash, and I poured them out right there on the counter and counted, one by one. Then I came back later and poured them out again, like a crazy person, and counted again. One by one. And there are fifteen missing! FYI, you are not supposed to take that many!!!"

I'm not sure that was very helpful.

And I'm not sure how helpful it was to follow him wherever he went and "catch" him in the act. Like the time I drove to the casino in the middle of the night and marched inside in my pajamas with my outdated, wire-rimmed glasses perched on my nose and my hair pulled into a messy bun on top of my head to have him *overhead paged.* I stood at the entrance, arms crossed, with my most exasperated face as he emerged with incredulous eyes as if to say, *"Really?!"* But I didn't actually say a word. I just turned on my heel and stalked out to the car. I may as well have hollered, "When we get home you're going straight to your room, young man!" Super helpful . . . though somehow it didn't change a thing.

And I'm not sure how helpful it was to print articles on pain medication or stimulants and their deleterious effects when used inappropriately (as if he didn't know). Or to remind him, over and over and over, he was using *drugs.* Which made him a *drug addict.* So he was surely a loser, and his behavior was ruining *everything.* Especially my perfect little plan for our lives.

What could he do when presented with this unceasing "help" and constant badgering except promise to stop? He promised that this was the last time. That he would do better now. He promised his desperate wife that life would somehow be *better* now.

Like an idiot, each time I believed him. Each time I bought in to his empty promises with my whole heart. And even though experience told me otherwise, I believed life would, in fact, be better now. And he would stop. I believed over and over he could control his drinking and drug use, and once he stopped, we could carry on with our regularly scheduled perfect little lives. I felt shocked and injured every single time my help didn't fix a thing and he continued to use.

So I quickly moved on to covering for him. Trying to make sure everything at home was just so. Trying to ensure he didn't miss a day of his rotations at the hospital. Calling and checking in. Lying to keep our devastating truth hidden from the world. And pretending everywhere we went that *everything* was fine. We're fine!! It's ALL fine!!!

I carried on with life as best I could on my own. Alone. Pressing forward with children and jobs and houses and friends. And all the while hiding our truth until, eventually, I was exhausted. All my worrying and pretending and carrying took its toll, and I was utterly exhausted, which left me angry. And bitter. And resentful. And *mean*. I hate to realize now how my unhealthy obsession caused me to miss out on so many of life's joys.

Somewhere along the way, I completely lost the ability to recognize where he left off and I began. And I was suffocating—taking everyone else in the family right along with me.

It would be years before I realized that his drug use wasn't really about me. His addiction was never, ever about hurting *me*. It was about his own pain. His own life. His own hurt. Every day he carried around the shame of destroying our family like a heavy weight on his back. He didn't need my cutting words. He didn't need my withering stares. He didn't need my lectures or my constant reminders about what a failure he was. My husband was absolutely drowning in life all on his own—yet over and over and over I stuck my foot on his forehead to push him under, and I held him there for a while as he struggled to come up for air.

It would be years before I realized he would have stopped if he could. Every day he woke with the intention that *this* would be the day. This would be the day he quit for good. And every single day he fell short as he was pulled further and further under the clutches of addiction while carrying all the weight of its guilt and shame. He just couldn't do it on his own. Addiction was out of his control. He was powerless over drugs and alcohol. And life had become unmanageable.

It would be years before I understood I was asking for things my spouse was incapable of giving at the time. Over and over I turned to him for love and friendship and confidence and trust. I yearned for a life partner who would know and accept the real me. Someone who wanted the same things I wanted. Someone working toward a common dream: the perfect life plan I crafted all those years ago. I wanted to depend on him. But for a long time, he was completely incapable of providing any of it for me.

It would be years before I decided to stop wasting so much time and effort and energy trying to control and change something and someone over which I had absolutely *no control*. My husband was responsible for his own life. And the best way to help was to get out of the way and allow life to bring its own consequences.

It would be years before I realized I had a choice. Day after day, *I have a choice*. And that choice is . . . me. My words. My actions. The level of mistreatment I am willing to put up with. And my own behaviors in response.

Al-Anon taught me a new way to live.

After years of Al-Anon meetings and small groups and countless books and coffee shop meetings with my sponsor, I learned a whole new way to look at life. I learned of changed attitudes and gratitude and realistic expectations. I learned of detachment and personal boundaries and forgiveness. I learned to concentrate on my own physical, mental, and emotional well-being and to realize, above all else, I could only focus on *myself*. Regardless of life's circumstances, I could be kind, listen well, speak my mind with respect, and let go of the results—even if it meant a life without my husband. Because really, the only person responsible for my well-being is me.

As we *both* worked through our problems, I had to admit right out loud to Dan that I hadn't been doing any of that—being kind, listening well, letting go—for a very long time. All our pain? Our life's problems? The total destruction of our perfect little plan? So much of it was my fault too. I had to make amends.

We lived apart for six months while my husband stayed in a three-quarter-way addiction recovery house as we each worked on our own lives, our own behavior, our own choices, our own recovery. And I considered this six-month period my time to learn how to live on my own. It was both extremely hard and absolutely lovely. Dan visited our home every evening for an hour or two to eat dinner and help put the boys to bed, but mostly he was away. The recovery house where he stayed had strict requirements for participation. He must be employed, he must attend daily AA meetings, he must do chores and be home by curfew. This time apart was so good for both of us.

I realized during this six-month period that starting a fresh life without him might be a fine option. I had already decided I would not live with active addiction again. Life with active addiction was too hard. And too painful. And not the life I wanted for my children. I wholeheartedly believed, now, that I was capable of living alone. I could do life as a single mom. I needed him—but I didn't *need* him.

Over our time apart, however, my husband's fog seemed to clear. And his eyes began to twinkle with life again. He showed up over and over exactly when and how he promised he would, and a little shred of hope pierced my heart. I was cautious. He was patient.

Our separation ended the very same week I finished my last day of family practice residency, which happened to be the very same time the house we were building (which I knew I could pay for with my new doctor's salary, and honestly assumed I'd live in as a single mom) was complete. Our move-in day? The night before Christmas Eve.

On the night before our official move-in, we dropped our two little boys at their grandparents' house and packed the Christmas tree and ornament boxes into the back of our Subaru for a date night in the empty living room of our new house. We wanted the tree to be up and decorated when we brought the boys home. Together. All four of us as a family.

We spread a blanket on the floor for a picnic under the glow of our new house's first Christmas tree. We hung all the ornaments and laughed and reminisced over every single one. Ornaments from our first married Christmas together. A clumsily made candy cane from our preschooler. Pictures in ornament frames of our little family from Christmases past.

Then right in the middle of it all, my newly sober husband paused for a moment and his eyes locked with mine as he wrapped his arms tightly around my waist.

"I want you to know, I'm sorry."

It was so different from the thousands of *sorrys* I heard in the past. This *I'm sorry* and the tears in his eyes said everything.

I'm sorry I missed so much—holidays, birthdays, milestones, trips to the park, family dinners.
I'm sorry you felt like you carried us.
I'm sorry for your sadness. Your pain. Your loneliness.
I'm sorry my addiction hurt you.
I'm sorry for all the times you felt afraid for our life together.
I'm sorry I left you alone.
I'm sorry I turned away from us.
And I am still here.

I let that sink in for a few moments as tears spilled down my cheeks. Then I hugged him tight. Because I had a whole long list of my own amends to make.

I was sorry for shutting him out.

I was sorry for making *everything* wrong with our marriage his fault.

I was sorry for his sadness. His pain. His loneliness.

I was sorry my behavior hurt him.

I was sorry for the times he felt afraid for our life together.

I was sorry I left him alone.

I was sorry I turned away from *us*.

And I am still here.

Then, right there on our empty living room floor, under the glow of our family Christmas tree, we made love like he had just emerged from the darkness. And as we lay together on the floor, all the pain and sadness and loneliness and resentment that gripped my heart for so long began to slowly and silently slip away as this incredible, life-changing forgiveness seeped in to fill all the holes and gaps.

I'm sorry changes everything.

I hadn't realized that all those months earlier, when God's love pulled me out of my dark pit, my husband had given up too. He reached his arms up and cried out for help just like I did. He called out to God in despair. *He surrendered.* And the same hand of LOVE pulled him right up out of that deep, dark, lonely pit. God pulled my husband out of his own rock bottom. We landed on opposite sides of the Grand Canyon. Miles and miles and miles apart. And over those next weeks and months and years, *love* showed us the way home. We stumbled and tripped and prayed and fell and crawled and clawed our way back together again. One day at a time. All the way around the rim of the canyon, we are finally reunited from out of the pit of pain and destruction—from the terrifying bottom alcohol and drugs flung us into.

For so long I was unsure we would go on together as a family. I wondered if I should just walk away. For years I'd been wading in the shallow end. Just dipping my toes. Living my life guarded and afraid. All those years ago I retreated to my own little corner, and I was terrified to jump back in. But that night years ago, amid Christmas and God's love and glowing lights and true love and *I'm sorry*, I plunged right into the deep end of our marriage once again. In a new house with a new job and a new perspective on life and love, together we began again.

> *If we are living and breathing, then we are always given the chance to get up and begin again.*

It turns out nothing in life is ever all lost. This beautifully flawed life is *never* pass/fail. In fact, I've been here for over forty years now, and I don't think I've ever really been given a grade. I want you to know, if we are living and breathing, then we are always given the chance to get up and begin again. We fail. We fall. We cry. We pray. We stand up. We dust off. We make amends. We say good-bye and move on to build our life anew. Or we decide to try again.[1]

For Dan and I, we're still here. And now *this* life is my favorite Love Story.

Prayer of Saint Francis of Assisi

LORD, make me an instrument of Thy peace.
Where there is hatred, let me sow love;
where there is injury, pardon;
    where there is doubt, love;
where there is despair, hope;
    where there is darkness, light;
    and where there is sadness, joy.
O, Divine Master, grant that
    I may not so much seek to be
consoled, as to console; to be
    understood, as to understand;
to be loved, as to love;
    for it is in giving that we receive,
it is in pardoning that we are
    pardoned,
and it is in dying that we are
    born to eternal life.

PART TWO

discovering beauty amid the rubble

SIXTEEN

forgiveness

Hurting and broken people often hurt other people. They don't always intend to, but sometimes their fear and sadness and hurt build up and begin to rise in their chests and bubble up through their ears until it all becomes so great that they spill out a bit of their unbearable pain onto everyone around them, especially the people they love.

I guess that's why a hurting and broken little girl might sometimes come home from school and close her bedroom door and scream obscenities at her beloved fluffy gray cat. Just to watch his ears lay flat. Just to make him feel small. Just to watch him cower in the corner. Because sometimes it feels better to let the pain boil over enough that all the fear and sadness and hurt can dull to a low simmer. But that's no way to live a life, simmering and rising and bubbling and finally spilling over onto anyone in your path. And that's where forgiveness comes in.

I spent many months in Al-Anon working toward healing in my marriage, forgiving my husband, making reparations in my relationships, and even, shockingly, learning to love myself.

Then my grandfather got sick.

My grandma had been gone for years, and when my grandfather quickly remarried, I didn't see him for a while. I hadn't seen him much at all growing up, actually—ever since the day I decided never to be alone with him again. Our relationship spent laughing and playing cards and his hilarious jokes and constant teasing were changed in an instant. And though I sent him an invitation, he didn't come to celebrate my wedding. My mother was angry, but I was relieved. I didn't really want to hug him in my white wedding dress.

I'd been married for almost nine years and had three children when I learned he was sick and surviving on a ventilator. Then when he transferred for more comprehensive care to a larger hospital in Omaha, it was only a few miles away from my home. So I decided I needed to go. I needed to say good-bye.

My aunts and uncles and cousins were gathered at the foot of his bed when I arrived, and we chitchatted for a few minutes before I asked if I could spend some time alone with him. His hospital room was so strangely quiet, with only the sound of machines whirring and beeping in the background, and I thought back to all those years ago, when I promised myself I would never be alone with him again. And yet, there we were. Alone again.

I sat on the edge of the bed next to his thin, pale frame, and for a long moment I was quiet. Then in a calm, steady voice, I said, "Grandpa . . . it's Mikki."

I think he raised his eyebrows just a little.

"I wanted to tell you . . . I'm married now. And I'm a doctor. I have three children. We just had our third boy, and I named him James. He's perfect."

And then . . .

"And I need you to know I'm okay. I'm not broken. You didn't break me. I've moved on . . . and I'm really happy. I have a good and wonderful life." I leaned over then and ever so lightly kissed his forehead as I whispered in his ear.

"And I am forgiving you."

I might have been lying that day. I've never really been sure. Was it true? Was it sincere? Forgiveness is such a tricky thing. But I *needed* to say those words. I needed him to know before he died. And I needed to tell him while I still had the chance, before he moved on forever from this earth.

Above all, I needed to remind *myself* that day—that I was okay. I wasn't broken. I had moved on with my life in many beautiful, wonderful, life-giving ways. I was happily married to a husband I adored while raising three beautiful babies, working at a meaningful and productive career, and enjoying an amazing and active sex life. All those awful things had happened to me, yes. They shaped me, yes. But those painful moments from when I was just a little girl never defined me. Those events *do not* define me.

I am okay. More than okay—I am whole.

He needed to know. I needed to know. There is forgiveness available for *all* of us.

Walking out of that hospital room, I felt lighter. Offering forgiveness and saying it out loud had reduced the simmer as I filled in yet another piece of myself I hadn't realized was still missing. I cried in my car in the hospital parking lot for a while before driving home to my beautiful family and my wonderful, ordinary life. I let the tears I'd been holding back for far too long fall freely. Tears to wash away all the pain and resentment and bitterness and any last remnants of fear. Tears because the difficult work of forgiveness is hard. *So hard.* And exhausting. And scary. And seemingly never-ending. But tears because I knew the difficult, exhausting work of forgiveness is *so good* too. And as I cried, I whispered through my tears,

"God, thank you. Thank you for helping me forgive. Please, help me to heal."

We try every type of bandage to cover old wounds, hoping to heal, don't we? We think, Maybe if I look just right? Or act just right? Maybe if I overachieve? Or outperform? Maybe if I shrink really, really small so no one will notice me? Maybe if I just . . . pretend?

We try it ALL.

We wrap and we tape and we cover with layer after layer as we pretend to be fine. We pretend it doesn't hurt anymore. And we heal, sort of. Though we tend to ignore that little bit of oozing blood and pus festering just below the gauze.

And really, it isn't until we finally pull off all the layers, rip off the bandage, and drag the painful truth kicking and screaming out into the open air that a scab can form. And with time, some new tender, pink new skin. And finally . . . a scar. A scar that will never quite be unnoticeable. A scar that will forever be in a state of remodeling. But for the first time, a scar that means we are intact. And whole.

Listen, I know all those layers seem like the only way. But maybe it's time to expose a few wounds so you can fully heal.

And I think it begins with forgiveness.

Though forgiveness *is* tricky, isn't it? Forgiveness seems nearly impossible sometimes. Because how do we forgive the unspeakable? The unthinkable? The unfathomable?

I have a little girl as I write this, and she is nearly the same age I was the very first time the unspeakable happened to me. My girl has the same hazel eyes. And the same messy, fly-away blond hair. And sometimes she laughs big and loud, and then she turns to me with those hazel eyes dancing . . . and I see myself. I don't want to. I realize she's not me. But sometimes I can't help it, and I do. I imagine I must've been just like her at that age. Small and sweet and innocent. And as I watch her playing and laughing and living and loving her life, every once in a while, a little question weasels its way into my brain.

Why? Why in the world would someone ever hurt a little girl? A small and sweet and innocent little girl? A perfect, unsuspecting little girl? And why does God stand back and allow that kind of hurt to take place? How?

Then the pit starts in my stomach. And the fear settles in. And before I know it, I realize I need to revisit forgiveness once again. Because the truth is, forgiveness is not a once-and-for-all thing. Sometimes it's an every-single-day thing. And even though we've done it before, every single time and every single day we revisit it . . . forgiveness is *hard*.

> *Forgiveness is absolutely the most challenging work we are asked to do down here.*

Forgiveness is absolutely the most challenging work we are asked to do down here. And though I've never been very good at it, I learned everything I know about forgiveness from Jesus. Our perfect example of how to forgive.

Often I can feel the weight of a cold, heavy stone in my hand as I can be so quick to condemn. *How dare she? How could he? What was she thinking? Doesn't he know?* And then my arm cocks back ready to cast my stone. *He deserves it.*

But in the very same breath, *Haven't I been her?* Haven't I been the woman with fingers of reproach wagging my direction, pointing to my pride and gluttony and lust and greed and comparison and lies and shame. Haven't I braced for the impact of cold, heavy stones hurtling my way? *Don't I deserve it?*

And in the middle of it all, I just can't stop thinking about Jesus. I can't stop picturing the way He stoops and draws in the sand, knowing every single thing about me. Knowing every one of my sins. He sees it all. Yet His body isn't rigid with hate or disgust. He doesn't grow angry. He'll never, ever pick up a stone, though He's the only one qualified to judge. Instead, He is kind and gentle and loving and merciful. He chooses love and grace for *every* sinner, the ones bracing for impact *and* the ones with cold, heavy stones in their hands.

I can feel His merciful eyes finally meeting mine when everyone else has tossed their stones aside and slowly trickled away.

"Go. And leave your life of sin."

It's all He has to say, though He knows full well I'll be back. Back to my sinful ways. Or back to pointing my fingers in reproach, ready to cast my stone. He knows. But He goes on loving me anyway. Forgiving me anyway. Waiting for me to return to Him again and again. Inviting me to put down my stone, let Him carry my hurts, and fold gently into His loving arms. Over and over and over. He is the model of forgiveness. He gave His life to carry *all* our sins, even the unspeakable sins against me. I am free to live and love and forgive because Jesus has already paid the price for *all* of us.

He waits. He stoops. He traces lines with His finger in the sand. Then He whispers gently, "I know, sweetheart. I'm here. I love you. Let it go. Forgive. I'll carry it all for you, my darling. Now you're free to go . . . and try again."

And I try.

Though sometimes one little word—the refrain to a song, or a movie, one teeny little trigger—flashes me right back to one of those moments out of nowhere. And I find myself as the little girl in the purple swimsuit all over again. Or the little girl on her rusty banana-seat bike with tears streaming down her cheeks, wondering what in the world must be wrong with her.

Sometimes my husband leans over to me in the dark and kisses me long and hard, and I *know* where this is heading. But instead of settling in and kissing him back, my stomach tightens. Then I have to remind myself, *You're okay. It's okay. It's DAN. You're safe here. With him. He loves you. No one is taking advantage of you.* Sometimes I have to grab the little girl inside of me firmly by the shoulders and smile and love and look her right in those hazel eyes and remind myself, *Sweetheart, you're OKAY! You are NOT this unspeakable thing that happened to you. You're not! Yes, it definitely shaped you. It affects your decisions. Your fears. Your inner voice. But this unspeakable, unthinkable thing DOES NOT define you. It might still scare you in certain situations. I know some of today's events will instantly bring you back to one of those past hurts. And I know how easily you revert to feeling small again. But you can overcome that. YOU WILL. You already have! And this one part of your story is not WHO YOU ARE. You are bigger. God is bigger.*

Forgiveness is not forgetting. Forgiveness is not condoning. Forgiveness *never* agrees there was no hurt or pain or ongoing consequences from an awful, unspeakable injustice. Forgiveness *never, ever* means I was not forever changed. But forgiveness is an absolutely essential path to fully healing. Jen Hatmaker puts it this way:

> The cost of forgiveness is high but the payoff is higher: health, peace, wholeheartedness, grace. It goes on: resilience, maturity, compassion, depth. God raises us back up mighty in love, through the pain, through the mess, stronger than before. Forgiveness does not erase your past—a healed memory is not a deleted memory—but it does enlarge your future, increase your love, and set you free.[1]

I'm not sure if I've forgiven, but I am forgiving my offenders. I am forgiving the people who failed to protect me. I am forgiving myself for carrying the shame and for keeping the quiet and for allowing the fear, for shouldering it all for so long. *I am forgiving.* Over and over and over, as many times as it takes.

And that's why I'm telling it now.

I want to honor the little girl in me. I want to honor anyone who might be holding tightly to something entirely too heavy to carry alone and struggling under the weight of unnecessary shame. I'm talking to *you* today. It's okay to put it down.

You can be happy.

You can be healed.

You can be whole.

And you have already been, every moment, *loved.*

It's okay to forgive. Because all that forgiveness? That over-and-over-every-single-day forgiveness? It's for *you and me,* really. Forgiveness is the daily choice we make to hand our cold, heavy stones to the Savior of the world . . . and be set free.

SEVENTEEN

dr. stay-at-home mom

We are constantly pushed to do more. Be more. Do it *all*. And many times, we *can* do more, so the guilt sets in as we regularly question, *Should I be doing more?* But just because we *can* do more doesn't mean we should. And the beauty is, oftentimes we get to choose. Here's how it went for me.

I always knew I would be a mom. And I fully intended to be a working mom. Working. *And* a mom. Super successful at both. You know, crushing the Mom thing and the Doctor thing all at the same time. Because women can do anything a man can do and then some, right?! I'm going to burn my bra! Tear down the establishment! The doctor is *IN*!

But then I delivered a few babies, and I watched it all with awe. I cried every single time. I'd be busy delivering the placenta or stitching up a perineal tear while stifling back a few tears because the whole thing was *all so beautiful*. New life is so breathtakingly beautiful! I still cry whenever someone sends me a picture of their newborn. And in medical school and residency when I was still delivering babies regularly, I yearned to be the fresh new mom in those first magical moments, pressing a bright pink squalling baby to my bare chest. More than anything else in the whole wide world, I wanted to be a *mom*.

The next thing I knew, I was one. And it was *me* holding my very first bright pink squalling baby to my bare chest, taking it all in with wonder and awe, as this time I could let the tears fall freely. My baby was here. And I became a *mom*.

If I'm being honest, I don't think I was ever fully present at my job again. My stomach twisted into knots leaving my babies every single morning. And even as we added another and another and another, leaving them never got easier.

I was always the one to stock the diaper bag and bottle up breastmilk and drop the boys at their grandma's before rushing off to work and then scheduling birthday parties on my lunch break. In between office visits (or occasionally while calling patients with lab results and simultaneously stuffing a sandwich into my mouth), I was pumping breastmilk and storing it away in the breakroom fridge. Turns out I couldn't burn any bras; I *needed* my bra to hold my breast pads in place so as not to leak all over my fancy button-down shirt.

No one ever told me it would be so hard. No one told me I wouldn't feel like I was killing it at anything ever again. No one told me I would feel like I was missing something every single moment. Not quite fully present with my patients while I was at work, but unable to push work completely out of my brain once I got home. I was forever trying to be two places at once—and often failing miserably.

No one told me I would constantly be in a hurry. Rushing to get up and get dressed and spend a few minutes with my babies in the morning. Rushing to get to work on time. Rushing through my day and stopping only to pump or call to check in on my babies (never enough time to even stop to pee). And finally rushing to get off work at a reasonable hour so I could speed to pick up my kids and get them home for dinner.

Home.

Home was where I longed to be. And for a few hours at home after a long day of work, I moved slowly. Meandering through dinner and our nightly walk and bath time. Savoring every moment. Rocking and cuddling and reading books to little boys piled on my lap and laughing and tickling and memorizing their little giggles and just *being a mom*. Then inhaling the tops of their heads at bedtime and trying to store away enough of them to get me through the next day, when I would have to leave for hours once again.

And after their bedtime, I went back to rushing. Rushing to get the laundry done, the dinner dishes loaded, the diaper bag packed, and everything ready for the next day. Rushing to get to bed on time so I could get up to do it all over again tomorrow. I was exhausted. I longed to slow down. In my oldest son's first year, I worked enough on-call nights at the hospital that I missed a full three months of his life. It broke my heart.

Why didn't anyone ever tell me about meshing my professional life with my new life as a mom? Why didn't anyone ever tell me how hard it would be to leave actual pieces of my heart, these little loves of my life, in someone else's hands for hours and hours of the day? Why didn't anyone ever mention the *guilt*? The constant pull between working and staying home with kids: the work guilt, mom guilt, wife guilt, "am I doing this right?" guilt.

I signed up for a career and put in all this hard work and effort and money and time to get the degree, and started at my very first job chasing after my dreams (more accurately, my *shoulds*). Then somewhere along the way, I had babies. And suddenly the demands of motherhood and family life and the sense of needing to be two places at once pulled me apart, and I was left shouting to the skies, *"GOD, WHAT AM I SUPPOSED TO BE DOING HERE???"*

I spent too many years living under the delusion that eventually I would arrive. Somewhere. To wherever I was endlessly chasing. The marriage. The fulfilling career. The family. The fancy home. And the perfect combination of balance between it all. It felt as though I had boarded a train that kept pressing forward and onward, and I couldn't get off, but I couldn't really see the destination.

Then, nine years ago, in the middle of all the doing and attaining and achieving and striving and trying to maintain balance, our family needed to move. Dan had been clean and sober going on four years when, during his last year of residency training to become a pathologist, he needed to do a year of fellowship training in Salt Lake City, Utah—one thousand miles away from family, friends, neighbors, my career, and the state I had lived in all my life. And because our move would likely be temporary, he casually mentioned I should just stay home with the kids for a while.

I will never forget my big, deep breath. My exhale. That releeeeeaaaase.

Home.

With my kids.

Unfortunately, that beautiful feeling lasted only a minute or two before my anxiety kicked in. *Move away? Where would we live? Where would the kids go to school? And what about their sports teams? What do you mean I could stay home? Do doctors do that? I am the breadwinner; how will we afford it? Cut our income by two-thirds? We have three children—how will we eat? And what about our family and friends? What will they think? Will we be able to sell our house in this market? HOW ARE WE POSSIBLY GOING TO DO THIS?*

I was so anxious about the whole thing, I considered staying behind with our three little boys to continue working while Dan moved to Utah to do his fellowship for a year. After all, it did make the most financial sense. But this idea felt like a punch in the stomach. I'd think about this plan and feel nauseated.

I prayed and prayed and prayed. *God, show me the way. Lead us and guide us. Please. Point out the path. Will you please tell me what to do?* Then one night while brushing my teeth, out of nowhere I broke down into sobs that wracked my body as toothpaste gushed out of my mouth and down my chin, and I crumpled to the floor.

Decision made.

Whether we lost money on the house or not. Whether I worked or not. Whether we lived in a house or a tent or our car, we would be going with Dan to Utah. Our family needed to be together. It was the only way.

In hindsight, I can easily see how God carried us through that time.

We sold our home in a losing market and broke even, then purged half our belongings, packed everything into one U-Haul, and moved a thousand miles away to the teeny-tiny house we rented in Bountiful, Utah.

We didn't buy anything except food for a year and spent all our free time hiking and exploring and riding bikes to the park or walking to the library for story hour. We lived on scrambled eggs or noodles and never went out to eat, although we did plant a garden and ate fresh tomatoes and zucchini and cucumbers from our yard. I woke early every morning for a run but left my timer and distance tracker behind. Then I'd come home to sit on the front porch and watch the hummingbirds flitting along the trumpet vine next to our driveway.

The beautiful feeling of release returned. And stayed. Every day I breathed in big and long and deep. Finally, I could breathe. I had stepped off the train. I watched it whiz by as I just stood there. Still and quiet. Feet planted firmly on the platform. Breathing in and out in long, slow, deep breaths.

Releeeeeeeaaaaaaase.

And nine years later we are still here. In Utah. I'm still mostly home and working only a shift or two a month. My days are quiet. I rush to soccer practice or basketball games, yes, but it all feels different now. Every single day I unwrap the precious gift of my deliciously slow, sometimes boring life. This beautiful, ordinary life. And for the first time, my outsides match the longings of my insides. For at least a few moments of every day, anyway.

I think most of us already know our right answer in our heart, and making a decision and moving forward is the hardest part. Because once we say it out loud and make it happen, we are finally free to breathe a sigh of relief.

This is *my* story, but there really is no one right answer.

I've been a working mom who averaged eighty hours per week working at the hospital with two kids under three at home while my husband was in and out of rehab. I've been a part-time working mom who averaged thirty hours per week with three kids under five at home while taking evening and weekend call and doing my own inpatient hospital work. And currently I'm working only one or two shifts per month while raising five kids from preschooler to teen. I still don't really know what the correct balance is! (And, yes, I realize what an incredible privilege it is that now I get to choose.)

Every single day I unwrap the precious gift of my deliciously slow, sometimes boring life. This beautiful, ordinary life.

You may decide you love your job and, even though every mom you see around you appears to be home with her babies as a seemingly perfect stay-at-home mom, you get so much fulfillment and joy in your career that you want to be able to do both. You can do it, sister!

You may decide that although you put so much effort into achieving a career and you have no idea how you'll survive financially without it, you feel like you are missing something at home every minute you are away, and you want more than anything to walk away from it all and raise your babies. You can do that too!

We will always struggle with doubt and insecurity at times. I do. A doctor who stays at home? Really? How will I ever be able to go back to it? And how many days per week can I work while somehow balancing the activities (and laundry) of five kids? I just *don't know*.

And then some days are *so awful* at home. I'm impatient. The kids fight, the house is a mess, and we're out of milk again. I forget to sign something for school, and I have no plans for dinner. Then I wonder, is this really what I am supposed to be doing? I'm so bad at it!

I get my answers in fits and starts.

Like one morning recently, as I sat next to my youngest in her little flannel Paw Patrol nightgown, her hair still a tangled mess of bedhead, I watched her slowly trace her index finger through the glob of peanut butter next to the apple slices on her plate. We had nowhere to go. Nowhere to be. No . . . rushing. She looked up at me in that moment and smiled a dimpled smile as her hazel eyes danced. And I exhaled once again in sweet release. Knowing so deeply, *I'm exactly where I'm supposed to be. Today.*

I'm realizing it doesn't have to be perfect. Every day won't be confirmation I've made the right choice, that's a guarantee. But for this season, I want to be home. I've decided I really don't care what other people think. I'm throwing away the *shoulds* of the world and I choose ME. I am reminded every day as my oldest boy tells me stories with his deep man-voice and towers above me or dunks a basketball in our backyard, this little season I'm in is *so very short-lived*. My kids are growing up! They will all be in school in one short year, and then I'll go back to working a few days a week. I still have decades to work outside the home.

As women, we have so many things we hope to accomplish in life, don't we? Sometimes it feels like we aren't making any progress. But truly I think we *can* achieve it all . . . just maybe not all at the same time. Balance is found over a lifetime. Every day I can only do the work I've been given to do *for just this day*. And listen. It's okay to put a few things down and choose a slower life. It's okay to pick up grace and hold it tight in your hands until you believe you are enough just as you are. No accomplishments needed. Please believe me when I say you don't have a single thing to prove.

Jennie Allen reminds us in her book *Anything* that we each get to do our own everyday and ordinary. What a gift.

> Godliness is found and formed in those places. No man or woman greatly used by God has escaped them. Great men and women of God have transformed the mundane, turning neighborhoods into mission fields, parenting into launching the next generation of God's voices, legal work into loving those most hurting, waiting tables into serving and loving in such a way that people see our God.
>
> Jesus says the way we glorify God, the way we step into his story, is by accomplishing the work God gives us to do.[1]

And everyone's story is different. Our days look different. Our contributions to the world are unique and can change over the course of one person's lifetime. My time for working and volunteering and running half marathons and traveling and mission work and all the rest is a little on the back burner for now as I'm raising five kids to adulthood. But in just thirteen more years, everything will change. Maybe working will be at the forefront. Or volunteering. Or this writing career I've been stifling for so long. Or any of the other million things I feel I've been called to do.

For me, this season is (mostly) for mothering. Yours may be completely different. And that's awesome! We each get to choose what the gift of our everyday, ordinary life looks like. For us. Let's pray about it. Follow our heart. Take a chance. And trust everything else will fall into place.

> Show me your ways, LORD,
>   teach me your paths;
> Guide me in your truth and teach me,
>   for you are God my Savior,
>   and my hope is in you all day long.
>
> Psalm 25:4–5

EIGHTEEN

an invitation

I've never been good at asking for help. And I've never been good at accepting help either, because in my mind, *"Perfect" people don't need other people.* Right? I can be such a slow learner. Thank goodness life offers us so many lessons!

A few months after my fourth baby, Luke, was born, I was determined to lose my baby weight. I wanted to get back into shape as soon as possible, and at the same time, I was longing to make a few friends. We'd been living in Utah for about a year, and I still felt like such a new girl here. I had a few acquaintances, but only one true girlfriend in the area. So when a mom from the church playgroup invited me to play on a women's indoor soccer team, I completely ignored how overweight and out of shape I was. I totally overlooked that this was a competitive league and that I hadn't played soccer for something like fifteen years. And I gave a resounding yes! Exercise and the chance to make a few new friends? Definitely YES!!

This little venture was incredible and amazing—at first. It felt so good to run again. After the first game, my sides were sore and my quads were sore and my lungs were sore, and it reminded me of returning to soccer conditioning every year in high school after taking the winter off. I was playing soccer again!

The games were from 9 to 11 p.m. on Wednesday nights, which made absolutely no sense for me because I was nursing a newborn baby around the clock and completely short on sleep. Also, every single player was at least five years younger than I, and I only knew one other person on the team. But still, it was so fun to play!

During the fourth or fifth game (of which I already had a hattrick, by the way), I was running back on defense to retrieve a loose ball when, just as I started to change directions with the ball, I felt someone run up behind me and kick me right in the calf. I heard a loud snap too. And instantly, I went down.

I turned around to see who would do such a horrible thing and realized there was no one there. I processed all of this information in about three nanoseconds:

OH NOOO!! I RUPTURED MY ACHILLES TENDON! It happened just like the textbook reads, "Feels like a kick in the calf . . . loud snap . . . instantly goes down and can't walk without falling forward . . . unable to plantar flex the foot." I'm going to need surgery! I'm going to be non-weightbearing for weeks!! I'M NOT GOING TO BE ABLE TO DRIVE! NOOOOOOO!!

After this little internal tirade, my teammates ran up to see if I was okay. I told them quite matter-of-factly that I had just ruptured my Achille's tendon. And I think I felt a few eyes roll in my direction like, *Lady, I think you're being pretty dramatic here. You probably just twisted an ankle. Stop being such a MOM!*

But nope, I was right.

I had ruptured my Achilles tendon. It was a complete tear requiring surgical repair and non-weightbearing status for four weeks with my right foot in a boot for a total of twelve weeks followed by physical therapy (which I'll admit I totally dropped out of), and no driving for the duration. Plus, the surprise result: one wimpy little right calf for life.

As a mother with four little boys at the time—two who already played sports, as well as a newborn who woke me a million times a night to be fed—plus a house to clean and laundry to do and groceries to buy and all the rest, this news felt impossible.

How in the world was I going to manage all of this?

No *driving*? Seriously? I may as well have had my leg amputated.

I posted this news on Facebook, of course. Because nothing really happens unless it appears on Facebook. Plus, I was looking for just a little sympathy from my faraway family and friends in Nebraska. And I never in a million years expected what happened next.

People started showing up for me.

Lots of people. People showed up to drive my kids to and from school. People showed up to get my kids to soccer or basketball practice. People showed up to drop off a gallon of milk. People showed up to force me out of the house for an hour at the church playgroup. People showed up to bring my family dinner—every night. *For a month*. I'm talking full meals with a main course, salad or side dish, and dessert. Every single night. I probably had thirty meals delivered to my house.

All provided, coordinated, and donated via women I had barely met. Other moms from school and women from church and women from the neighborhood and moms from my kids' sports teams and new friends from playgroup. Everybody just showed up. Offered help. Called or texted. Lent a hand. Provided dinner. Day after day after day. My treasured college girlfriends from afar even hired me help with housecleaning for a month. An amazing team of two women came every two weeks with their cleaning supplies and scrubbed toilets and washed floors and dusted blinds and changed bedsheets. My house was gleaming and spotless that month (and it hasn't really been that clean since).

Do you know what I was busy doing that month of non-weightbearing in my clunky black boot?

I was wearing sweatpants. I was sitting on my couch and snuggling my newborn baby. I was reading books to my preschooler. Or napping when my littles napped. My only jobs included dressing us and painstakingly making my way down the stairs on one good leg while holding a baby so we could sit on the couch for the rest of the day. I didn't have to drive kids to school or cook or clean or grocery shop or cart kids off to soccer practice. I simply sat. And healed.

And do you know the most beautiful result from this entire experience?

These women are my girlfriends to this day. The true girlfriends I longed for and craved! Suddenly, I didn't feel much like the new girl anymore. Instead, I felt loved and adored and connected and special and cared for. Suddenly, I belonged. Here in Utah. With them. And these women remain my go-to girls when I'm in a jam. I call them when I'm feeling stressed or have some important and exciting news or just need to hear a friendly mom-voice on the other side. Sometimes, I list my friends Annie or Diana as my emergency contacts because I don't truly have any family nearby and they are like family to me. When my nanny situation fell apart while I was still working regularly, these women stepped up immediately to help watch the kids while I finished out my last weeks of work. Nearly every month of the last school year before the pandemic, my friend Tina came to watch my kids for no reason at all. She just wanted to give me some time to myself. When I need company and haven't been out of the house without kids for a while, these women join me for dinner and we laugh and talk until our ears practically fall off. And my Nebraska friends do the same once a year on our annual girls' trip.

I didn't realize it at first, but my broken Achilles tendon was an invitation, really. An invitation to slow down a little more and live. An invitation to ask for help and then actually stand back (or sit on my couch in sweatpants) and allow others to help me for once. It was an invitation to *let go* and be loved. It was another of life's reminders that I don't have to do it all alone.

Then 2020 began.

For a while, 2020 had me believing I would never be happy again. My habit of picking up all the hard things and carrying everything on my own (plus sometimes sweeping up everyone else's problems while I'm at it) ramped up in full force. The pain, the uncertainty, the growing numbers, the news, the monotony, the unemployment rates, the fighting,

My broken Achilles tendon was an invitation to slow down a little more and live.

the sadness. Many times during 2020 I felt so alone, even though every other person in the world was going through some version of the same thing.

When coronavirus showed up at our house for the Christmas season, our whole family had fevers and chills and body aches, and my husband and I lost our taste and smell by Christmas Eve. And life felt hard. I started wondering, *God, where are You?*

But then once again, people started showing up for me.

My dearest friend from Nebraska called almost daily to ask, "How are you today? Are you surviving?" like she has for every single hard thing that has ever come my way. A neighbor from up the street left a fancy breakfast spread of pancakes and orange juice and cartons of raspberries and blueberries on our doorstep. The pancakes were still warm from the stove, and I've never felt so loved! Those same friends who cared for me all those years ago when I ruptured my Achilles tendon delivered Papa Murphy's pizza or broccoli cheese soup or enchiladas and even a little gingerbread house kit for the kids. And I remembered, again, that I am *never* alone.

My village came and surrounded my family (socially distanced, of course). And as my fever broke and the brain fog cleared, I realized, *He's right here.* He's *always* right here. There is goodness even here. Even now. In me and her and our neighbors and that guy over there and you.

I suppose "perfect" people don't need other people, that's true. But I'm learning again and again that perfectly *ordinary* and flawed human beings do. And that's all of us, isn't it? That's me and you!

If we are paying attention, our invitations come one after the other in this life. Invitations to show up and lend a hand and accept help and serve others and truly *live* together in this one precious, beautiful life we've been given to live. Exactly the way He has planned. We only need to open our ears to hear, our eyes to see, our hearts to understand . . . and say *yes!*

NINETEEN

on the run

A year or so after I ruptured my Achilles tendon, I signed up to run a half marathon. I'd run a few of these races before, but this would be the first one following my surgery, the truest test of whether I'd fully healed from my injury.

With four kids and all their activities and a house to run and a toddler to tend to, I had almost no time to train (and a lot of excuses, obviously). But I ran a few miles several times a week, and once a week I forced myself to go on a long run. When race day came, the longest training run I'd done was only eight miles—nowhere near the 13.1 miles I'd need to run in order to complete the race.

But I was determined to try it anyway.

During training, my dear friend Amy, who also likes to run, suggested I do what she'd done during her first half marathon: choose thirteen people to think about and focus on and pray for during each mile of the race, and run the entire race *for* someone. I could run this race for my loved ones. I thought this sounded like a fantastic idea, so as I trained, I also constructed my list. I could only choose thirteen people.

On race day, I woke early and ate a healthy breakfast and rode the train to the starting line with a few mom friends from the neighborhood. Then, when the race began, my visualization and prayer began too.

I ran a mile for each of my children. And as I ran, I thought about the day each was born. I thought about their amazing personalities and my hopes and dreams for each one as they grow. I prayed over them and asked Jesus to be present in their lives. I asked Jesus to lead them and guide them and hold them every single moment of every single day of their lives.

And I cried.

I ran for my husband. I thought about the day we were married. I thought about all those hard years. I thought about visiting him in rehab. I remembered the night we decided to begin again there under the lights of our Christmas tree in our new house. I thought about what an amazing man he's become. And how proud I am to do this life with him and call him my husband. I realized how, with every year, my love just grows and grows and grows. I prayed over him and our marriage and our little family. I asked Jesus to be present in our lives. To lead us and guide us and hold us every single moment of every single day of our lives.

And I cried.

I ran for my mom.

I ran for my family and friends, each as a collective group.

I ran and ran and ran.

I ran for a little baby I cared for in the NICU who was born to a drug-addicted mother. Born a fighter, battling lung issues and infection and seizures, he was instantly a ward of the state. During the month I spent caring for him, I took every chance I could to feed him and rock him and sing him the same songs I sang to my little boys at home. As I ran, I wondered about where he might be now. I imagined what he might look like as

143

a ten-year-old boy. I prayed he might live with an adoptive family who loves him. I prayed he was safe and warm. I prayed for friends for him and a good school and plenty of food to fill his tummy. I prayed that he will always, always feel loved. I asked Jesus to be present in his life. To lead him and guide him and hold him every single moment of every single day of his life.

I ran for a beautiful woman named Abby who died of cystic fibrosis during my month working in the ICU. I thought about how she looked at me in those last few moments before the respiratory team came to intubate her and asked, "Am I going to die??" and how I answered her as honestly as I could: "We're going to do everything we can . . . and I'll be right here the whole time." And I was.

I ran for Joshua. He came to see me for only a few months after his stay in rehab, and I knew what that meant. I wondered if he ever found sobriety. I prayed he found Jesus.

I ran for Lanae, a woman I eventually let go from my care for screaming at my nurses and behaving inappropriately at the clinic. I thought about her rough life being raised by a drug-addicted mother and how she never learned to read, and the way in which she was attempting to raise babies of her own. All on her own. I'd done my very best to take care of her, but I could never possibly imagine walking a day in her shoes, so I ran for her instead.

And I cried. And I prayed. And I ran.

Then on the thirteenth mile . . . I ran for Kindra.

My lungs burned and my legs ached, and I knew already I was going to be *so sore* because I hadn't adequately trained for this thirteen-mile race, and I wanted so badly to walk. I wanted to quit.

But I ran anyway.

I ran because Kindra never got the chance to run as much and as far and as fast as her legs should have carried her. I ran because she spent her last few years in a wheelchair. I ran because she never got to see her baby become a little boy and run and jump and laugh. She didn't have enough chances to lift him above her head as he screamed with delight, then bring him down to bury her nose in his neck, making him squeal with laugher. She never got to watch him walk on his own little legs into kindergarten or catch his first fish or play soccer.

I ran for Kindra.

And, my God, how I cried.

I prayed God has given her a special place in heaven. And that she might be able to watch her boy grow from the very best seat available. I prayed I will remember her every day when I am tired or grumpy or bored or exhausted and wishing for a break from my children.

I ran for her.

And at the very close of the race, during the last tenth of a mile toward the finish line when my legs began to feel numb . . .

I ran for *me*.

I ran for the little girl in the purple swimsuit. And the little girl on the banana-seat bike. I ran for the girl who buried her hamster wondering why God had forsaken her. I ran for the girl who spent her whole life trying to get inside the Circle. Trying to please people. Trying to look a certain way and act a certain way. Attempting to be *perfect*. I ran for the woman who finally learned one day to stop pretending and really *live*. I prayed for her. I prayed for Jesus to be present in my life. To lead me and guide me and hold me every single moment of every single day of my life.

I am strong. And my story is beautiful. This life is beautiful.

And I cried.

I ran and cried and ran and cried.

And I finished the race! So tired. And so unbelievably *proud* of it all.

During my run, I was reminded I am strong. And my story is beautiful. *This life* is beautiful. It is hard and lovely and messy and gritty and breathtaking and heartbreaking and *beautiful* . . . and we each have our own race to run.

So come on, let's put one foot in front of the other. And even if we cry the whole way, let's run!

TWENTY

just one more

My fourth child was born approximately four minutes after I made it into the delivery room. I was still wearing my shirt and had barely ripped off my pants while my husband struggled through the door carrying all our bags in his hands. There was absolutely no time for my planned epidural when, amid *much* profanity mixed with just a little bit of screaming, there he came. Our Luke.

The doctor held my dimpled baby boy high in the air as she exclaimed, "Mikala, it's okay! He's here!" And Dan's first words were, "THAT . . . WAS . . . AWESOME!! That was just like the movies!!"

I responded with, "I will *never* do that again."

But my husband just smiled as he replied, "Never say never."

I thought we were done after four. Four was *always* the number. Four was part of the plan. My plan. And we had four healthy, active little boys. I had settled quite nicely into my role as a Boy Mom. I donated all the baby gear —the stroller, the car seat, the ExerSaucer, and the highchair. I gave away all my maternity clothes. Luke was the sweetest and happiest and smiliest toddler I'd ever known. And we bought a dog. We really *tried* to be done. Plus, at thirty-six years old, I technically qualified for advanced maternal age.

But I kept feeling these little nudges. So often I heard the faintest little whisper, *Just one more.* And I saw glimpses wherever I went of the little girl missing from our family. One day I'd see a little girl with long, tangled, sandy blond hair pulled back into a ponytail on the soccer field. Another day I'd notice a little girl skipping along next to the cart at Target with her mom, chattering all the way. And every time I'd think briefly to myself, *I bet my girl would've been a lot like that.*

Then one day a few years ago, I went out for a run and let my mind drift there. . . .

Her name would have been Elizabeth Grace. She would have had sandy blond hair and my hazel eyes. And dimples. She would have loved babies. And bugs. And she would have had the world's best laugh. And the world's biggest and brightest personality. She would have been fearless. And wild. And sweet.

I could see her so clearly. My girl. And I realized it wasn't another baby I wanted—it was her.

Lizzy.

Halfway through my run that day, as my mind swirled with thoughts of the baby girl who was missing from my life and this family, I stopped. I doubled over against my knees to catch my breath and choked back a few audible sobs. And in that very moment I knew.

We would have one more. And it would be *her.*

Once home, I marched into the kitchen with tear-stained cheeks, still hot and sweaty from my run, and announced to my husband, "We *have* to have one more!" He looked a little surprised because this announcement seemed to come out of nowhere. But he just smiled and quickly agreed. Because honestly? I think he always knew she was coming too.

Then one night, weeks later, I leaned over to him and said something like, "If you're not sure you want another baby, then you better stay far away from me." Which meant he pounced almost immediately. And I knew instantaneously that I was pregnant. Before I closed my eyes that night, I whispered just this one small prayer: *"Dear God, can it please be HER?"*

I wasn't even surprised at the ultrasound. Because I already knew. I'd been waiting for her.

Today Lizzy is five. I've had five years with this beautiful little creature. Five years with my little girl, who has sandy blond hair and the world's *biggest* personality. I'm still a little surprised sometimes to find bursts of pink next to all those mesh basketball shorts in the laundry. Or stumble over baby dolls and toy bottles or mini-spatulas and dollhouse pieces all over the floor. There were just so many years of boys!

But every single day I'm grateful. I'm so grateful I listened to those little whispers.

Just one more.

Lizzy grounds me. She keeps me present and *right here* in a whole new way. She is full of questions about life and her body and babies and puppies and the world in general. She follows me wherever I go.

"Momma, can I sit on your lap?"

"Momma, will you play babies with me?"

"Momma, can I help you with that?"

"Momma, can I come with you?"

"Momma, where are you?"

"Momma, what are you doing?"

"Momma, will you carry me?"

"Momma, I just need you!!"

"Momma, will you lay with me?"

"Momma, will you snuggle me for one more minute?"

Momma.

Momma.

Momma.

She always, always wants to be right by my side. And just when I want to escape with a book or a new recipe or a little mindless Pinterest or a phone call to a friend, she pulls me back.

"Momma?"

On her last birthday I snuggled next to her in the dark as her little star nightlight lit up the ceiling, and I couldn't stop fat, warm tears from rolling down my cheeks and splashing onto her little turquoise floral pillow. I breathed her in and quietly realized I might never have known how to wash little girl hair. Or how to comb it gently into curls. I might never have twisted wispy blond hair back with bright pink or yellow bands into itty-bitty piggies or buns. Or painted tiny toddler toes a raspberry pink to match my own with her adorable exclamation, "I haf pink tooooeees, just like Mommy!" I might never have patted silky pink princess pajamas while rocking her in the corner rocking chair of the nursery and singing "You Are My Sunshine" or "Amazing Grace" every night. And I might never have heard my daughter's sweet voice whisper in the dark as she wraps her little arms around my neck and presses her nose against my nose, her sweet breath warm against my face, "Momma, we're best friends. Right?"

I know without a shred of a doubt . . . my Father in heaven truly gives good gifts to those who ask Him.

Each night as I quietly tuck her into bed, I lean gently toward her soft cheek and whisper, "I'm so glad you're here. I'm so glad God chose *me* to be your mom."

And you know, sometimes she turns to me with those dazzling hazel eyes, and she laughs the world's *best* laugh. And her dimples flash. And I know. I *know* without a shred of a doubt . . . my Father in heaven truly gives good gifts to those who ask Him. In fact, over and over and over He gives me everything I never knew I always needed. And I'm so grateful. I'm grateful for a God who sends us healing and answers in the unlikeliest of places. We pray. We wait. We listen. We believe. And sometimes, if we're lucky, we get exactly what we've been searching for all along.

I'm so grateful for this little girl. For *her*.

Lizzy, I was waiting, my darling.

Ask and it will be given to you; seek and you will find; knock and the door will be opened to you. For everyone who asks receives; the one who seeks finds; and to him who knocks, the door will be opened.

Matthew 7:7–8

TWENTY-ONE

our very fine house

We need Joy as we need air. We need Love as we need water. We need each other as we need the earth we share.

—Maya Angelou

We're living in a house that I never expected would be our Forever Home but more like a We-Need-To-Move-Somewhere-Quickly-Because-Our-Lease-Is-Up-On-Our-Rental-And-I'm-About-To-Have-Another-Baby Home.

This house has certainly served us very well over the years, but it's in the kind of neighborhood where if you accidentally turned down the wrong street, you wouldn't notice. And you might walk into the wrong house because every house looks exactly like every other house on the block. Also, our yard is small. Every five minutes my kids are climbing a fence to grab a ball that has gone into the neighbor's yard because just one throw or hit or toss or whack sends each and every ball over the fence. Oh, and now we have *five* kids. The oldest towers over me by several inches and all three of my biggest boys have gigantic stinky feet. Let's just say we are seriously outgrowing things around here.

So, because of the cookie-cutter look and small yard and exponential growth of our family, I started looking at new houses. We walked through several open houses. We scoured the Zillow feed. We drove around and snooped in backyards and peeked through windows.

After weeks of searching, I found one that seemed practically perfect. It was situated just a few blocks from our favorite hiking spot in the mountains on one flat acre. It was almost twice the size of our current home and had a basement (a much-needed space for my teen boys, who could really use a man-cave when their friends come to hang out). I loved the roomy, updated kitchen and wood floors and open floor plan and big picture windows and landscaped yard and amazing neighborhood. It was a *gorgeous* home.

But it was super expensive.

How could I justify a house that would be more than *double* the cost of our current home?

My mind went back and forth. I lost hours of sleep over it. I envisioned where we might place all our furniture in the new house, and realized we'd have to buy a lot of new furniture. And rugs. And a fence for the dog. I also realized I would want to remodel a few bedrooms *and* a bathroom *and* the basement kitchen area. Oh, plus the deck off the kitchen on the back probably needed to be replaced.

More money. More time. More resources. More on my to-do list. More anxiety.

The day after our walk-through was a Sunday, so I packed up all my kids and all my anxiety and headed to church. I knelt to pray and felt called to ask God for help. It went something like this:

God, I'm so sorry I am such a spoiled brat. I'm sorry I am NEVER content with what I've been given. You've answered so many of my pleas. A sober husband. A healthy family. The chance to stay home with my kids for a while. I'm so sorry I am continually looking for the next thing that I think might make me happy. Can you forgive me? Can you help me to be content? I don't want to move and spend more money and remodel rooms and buy all new furniture. I just want to be content with EXACTLY what I have.

Then the bell announcing the beginning of Mass rang, and I stood and turned toward the back of the church. I realized right away we had a visiting priest. And as he started Mass and introduced himself, I was awestruck that my prayer had been answered. Already. Only about thirty seconds after I uttered that silent prayer begging God to help me find contentment, this was my answer.

Our visiting priest was from the Food for the Poor outreach program, and he spends his life serving the poor and starving and sick and dying people in countries like Guatemala, the Dominican Republic, Haiti, Nicaragua, El Salvador, and Honduras.

He spoke to us of his life's ministry work. He showed us pictures of starving children and families living in trash heaps. He told us there are truly only five things necessary in order to live a meaningful and productive life: food, clean water, shelter, education, and medical care. He explained to us how life-changing a new home for one of these families would be for them. And he absolutely answered my prayer.

I will never forget watching my children's faces as they stared long and hard at the starving children in those pictures. "Mom, we should pay to build them a house."

Now, on this particular Sunday, my husband had decided his "church" would consist of trail running in the mountains. So when I got home from the church service led by the Food for the Poor priest, I marched straight into the kitchen with the kids and said to Dan, "I don't want a new house. Spending that much money on a house feels . . . bad. I want to live *here*. Forever. All I need is a back patio and a kitchen backsplash . . . and maaaaybe a big, white farmhouse sink." Then I explained my experience from our morning in Mass. I showed him pictures of the starving families living in trash heaps. And just as I paused for a moment to catch my breath, my husband quickly interrupted, "Well, what are we waiting for? Let's build a house!"

God, thank you for giving me a kind and generous husband who understands me.

Today, sometimes when I'm walking around picking up toys off our dingy rug for the millionth time or debating what I'm going to make for dinner (why is dinner *every* night??), I notice how much I love the way the light filters through the blinds into our living room during the late-afternoon sunshine while the sky outside turns an orangey-pink.

I think about how blessed I am to have this beautiful family in our ordinary little house in an ordinary neighborhood with clean water and plenty of food stocked in our kitchen pantry and gallons of milk in the fridge. Then I say a prayer of thanks as we all sit down together around our worn dining table, and I serve nutritious (okay, nutritious-ish) food to fill their tummies.

Some mornings, I sit outside on our new back patio and watch the hummingbirds chase and flit and chirp around the feeders hanging along the back fence. I check the veggies growing in the garden or water the flowers blooming on our front steps.

I pick wet towels up off the floor in our bathroom (again) and think about the school where I drop the boys every day to learn and the doctor's office or pharmacy up the road should any of us get sick. And I can't help but smile as I pass by the jar on the dresser where my fifth-grader is saving spare change for a water pump for one of the Food for the Poor families who need it.

I shove laundry from the washer to the dryer to the big soaking sink in our laundry room (where those clothes will sit until someone comes to dig through and wear them because our laundry never actually gets folded). And I just live my one beautiful, ordinary life in my ordinary, cookie-cutter house. True, it looks nothing like I once imagined it "should." But this house is all I'll ever need. It's even more beautiful as I remember the lovely family living in the house we funded in Guatemala.

I pray for them. Often.

And I am grateful. Most days, I feel so unbelievably content with *exactly* what I have. My beautiful, messy family in my utterly ordinary life. What an amazing gift that Guatemalan family gave to me. The gift of contentment. Isn't it amazing how we all just *need* each other?

What if every day we remember to live contentedly with exactly what we have?

God, I'm so unbelievably grateful for this meaningful, productive life. Thank you for showing me how to be content. I'm especially grateful for our new kitchen back-splash after waiting eight years, and for the people in my life who remind me of everything I really NEED. Amen.

TWENTY-TWO

this perfect stranger

Several years ago, my dear friend Amanda sent me the book *Carry On, Warrior* by Glennon Doyle. I read the whole thing cover to cover in two days. I couldn't put it down. When I finished the book, I immediately turned to the front and started reading again. Near the beginning, there's a chapter where Glennon invites her readers to write:

> If, anywhere in your soul, you feel the desire to write, please write. Write as a gift to yourself and others. Everyone has a story to tell. Writing is not about creating tidy paragraphs that sound lovely or choosing the "right" words. It's just about noticing who you are and noticing life and sharing what you notice. When you write your truth, it is a love offering to the world because it helps us feel braver and less alone. . . .
>
> Just do it. Be generous. Offer a gift to the world that *no one else can offer: yourself.*[1]

As I reread this section, I flopped the book down on my chest and immediately burst into tears. Because this book, right here, was how I'd *always* wanted to write. I considered Glennon's words to be yet another invitation in my life: to start showing up to a gift and talent I'd always loved. I knew she was speaking right to *me*. And as I bawled a shoulders-shaking kind of cry and hugged her beautiful book to my chest, I whispered aloud to my living room, "I have *so many* stories to tell."

So naturally I did absolutely nothing about it. I sat on this idea for years. Occasionally I'd write a super-lengthy Facebook post and a few people would comment, "You should start a blog!" I always just laughed at this idea and brushed it off, thinking, *Who, me? I'm not a writer.*

But then one day I boarded a plane with a Jen Hatmaker book in my hand. (Sidenote: I once told a writer friend my greatest writing goal would be to sit on Jen Hatmaker's porch with Glennon and Jen, eating chips and salsa and celebrating the release of my new book—so, in other words, I kind of admire them both!) Anyway, I was headed for our annual girls' trip to a lake in North Dakota with my college girlfriends. And as I plopped down in my airplane seat, I accidentally sat on the seatbelt of the woman beside me. Then as we fidgeted around in our seats and untwisted straps and passed buckles back and forth to one another, we struck up a conversation. And for two hours and twenty-five minutes we talked nonstop and barely came up for air. It turned out she has four boys and I have four boys with a baby girl at the caboose. So that's how we got started, with pleasantries.

But very quickly our conversation shifted to life and relationships and careers and aspirations and the pain in our past and so many very intimate details of our lives—all being passed back and forth between perfect strangers. I told her *everything*. My whole life story. The flight attendant had to interrupt us when she passed out the snacks, and I bet the poor girl trying to nap against the window in the third seat of our row was so annoyed.

Here were my initial impressions that instantly drew me to this lovely woman: She is confident and self-assured. She is deeply rooted in her faith. She is an amazing mom to her four boys, loving them fiercely but giving them room to grow. And she is the world's *greatest* encourager; encouraging others is obviously her gift from God.

At one point, our discussion turned to what I *really* wanted to be when I grew up. A writer. She turned to me with all seriousness and looked me straight in the eyes as she replied, "Oh, but Mikala, you *are* a writer!" Then she pulled out an imaginary piece of paper and with her imaginary pen wrote with gusto on an imaginary diploma, "You Are a Writer." Then she handed it to me with confidence. I pretended to take this imaginary piece of paper from her hand, and for the rest of the ride I sat with my diploma in my lap.

This lovely stranger had declared it to the world. *I am a writer.*

Would you believe my new friend lives on a farm with her husband, but she works traveling as a motivational speaker? Obviously. And isn't it something she had the seat right next to mine on an airplane with my Jen Hatmaker book in my hand?

At the end of our flight, we exchanged information. We walked down the Jetway together and hugged good-bye. I was so sad to see her go. When I met up with my girlfriends outside the airport, I told them, "You guys, I just met this woman on the plane. We became friends immediately. It was the strangest thing. I felt like I knew her. I actually *hugged* her good-bye. Is it weird I already friended her on Facebook?" And they did look at me like I was a little bit crazy. Then we spent a lovely weekend together on the lake.

The evening I got home from that trip, I started a blog. A whopping thirty-nine family members and friends signed up. And that teeny little blog was the beginning of a teeny little dream that eventually became the book you're holding in your hands.

My new friend and I still message each other once in a while. She told me all about her son leaving for college. She had some medical concerns, and I prayed for her health and safety. I messaged her when I had my first article published somewhere other than my own little blog. She shared my very first viral piece. And whenever I see a comment from her on one of my writings, I smile this big, wide smile. I'm so proud to have her read it. I am truly grateful for this woman. I believe God plopped me right next to her on that plane for a reason. He nudged. And nudged. And nudged. I had so many invitations through the years. But then He began to shout and holler through the encouragement of this lovely woman on a plane. God sent this *perfect* stranger to collect my RSVP. I could almost hear Him asking, "Honey, you know what I'm asking you to do. I've given you this talent and a little dream in your heart. And I'm waiting, sweetheart. Are you going to listen?"

So now I write.

I write at 5 a.m. while the house is quiet or in the car waiting for kids to finish soccer practice. I write in my bathtub after the kids are asleep or on the side of the track at the gym. I write in the middle of the night because I can't sleep until I write the words that are constantly running through my brain.

It's the first time in my life I've done something just for me. Just because. It's the first time in my life I've done something not because I *should* do it, but because I *want to*.

Writing is a gift I've been waiting to unwrap my entire life. It lights me up and fills my heart and brings me so much joy! Even if no one else ever reads it or likes it or shares it.

Did you realize we can do that? We can write or paint or dance or sing or garden or bake not because we'll make a ton of money. Not because we have all this extra time on our hands. Not because anyone ever asked us to. Not because we *should*.

We can create for no other reason than we *want to*—just for the love of it. Because God gifted us with particular talents and interests. Because it fills our hearts and brings us joy. Because it makes us feel ALIVE! And He truly delights when we listen to His nudges and feed our unique passions.

We can create for no other reason than we want to—just for the love of it.

Beautiful writer and spiritual teacher Elizabeth Gilbert says,

> A creative life is an amplified life. It's a bigger life, a happier life, an expanded life, and a . . . more interesting life. Living in this manner—continually and stubbornly bringing forth the jewels that are hidden within you—*is* a fine art, in and of itself.[2]

She is so right.

I write because it reminds me, I'm a whole person outside of being a wife and a mom and a doctor and a daughter and a sister and a friend. I'm a *me*. And I love to write. I absolutely *love* bringing forth the jewels that are hidden in my chest and sharing my truth with the world. It is my unique love offering, just like Glennon said. The gift of *myself*.

And I know you have your own passion to share.

What's your gift? What's your little hidden surprise? Won't you share what's inside you?

The world is waiting, my friend. Consider this your invitation. God is gently nudging. He has given you a talent and a dream in your heart. Are you going to listen? I'm here to collect your RSVP.

TWENTY-THREE

uncurated

There is no way to be a perfect mother and a million ways to be a good one.

—Jill Churchill

A mom of four came to my clinic one day with a swollen, purple finger poking out from an ACE wrap bandage as she looked at me with shame and tears in her eyes.

"I think I broke my finger."

"What happened?" I asked, unwrapping the bandage and examining her finger.

I could tell she didn't really want to say it out loud. So I remained quiet. I waited. There is so much power in the wait.

"I was just so ANGRY!!!" she nearly shouted to the room.

Then it all came spilling out. She'd been *fed up* with her kids that morning. The bickering. The fighting. The talking back. The not listening. Then, in a fit of Mommy Rage, she slammed her book down on the kitchen table as hard as she possibly could. You know, to make her point. Only her hand was so close to the edge, the book slipped off and she slammed her finger down on the table instead. Hard enough to fracture the bone.

She looked so ashamed.

"What kind of mother gets so angry with her children that she breaks her own finger?" she cried, her face brimming with guilt.

Her eyes looked at me imploringly. I could tell she had convinced herself she was the only one. The *only* mother who ever loses her temper. Slams things. Yells. Says things she doesn't mean. Breaks her own finger. I wondered if she'd done a Google search before she came. *Does breaking my own finger in a fit of rage make me a bad mom?*

I gave her my very best you-are-not-alone look.

"But do you love them?"

"With all my heart!!!" was her emphatic reply.

"And have you ever actually physically hurt your children?"

"Well, of course not!"

I just smiled. "You're a great mom. I can tell."

Then I sent her off for an X-ray.

We're told from the very beginning that life is supposed to be beautiful. Motherhood, in particular, is *supposed to be* beautiful. And with all the helpful Pinterest pins and those shiny Instagram filters and the endless articles titled "Moms Who Do These Five Things Raise Happy Kids," mothers are constantly given the impression that motherhood should be beautiful *all* the time. Like we should walk around in a permanent state of bliss marveling at our perfect children and in awe of our astoundingly beautiful lives. And if it isn't perfect and beautiful, we should probably try a whole lot harder to make it so. Right?

I'm just as guilty as all the rest.

Before I had kids, I bought in to this story wholeheartedly. I read all the books: *What to Expect When You're Expecting,*

Babywise, The Five Love Languages for Children, The Baby Whisperer, Parenting with Love and Logic. And of course, I planned to use the extensive knowledge I gained from all these informative books to do it all perfectly.

My motherhood would be *so* beautiful!

I would breastfeed for at least a year and have my children on impeccable sleep schedules and raise babies who were born loving all fruits and vegetables and eating everything on their plates. My children would somehow be both incredible athletes and near-genius readers. I'd raise the world's most elite prodigy children. And I would never, ever lose my temper. Motherhood was obviously going to be another place for me to thrive. And then I'd line up all my beautiful memories into perfect little squares and top them off with shiny Instagram filters for everyone to see.

How beautiful!

But then *real* motherhood kicked in and I had to throw all my plans right out. Because those perfect, shiny images we see on social media aren't presenting the whole truth, are they? That's not *real* motherhood, is it? Social media is wreaking havoc on motherhood, you guys!

But sometimes I find myself scrolling anyway.

And as I scroll along, looking at everyone else's shiny lives, I might notice a mother who has all these wonderful things to say about her children. And motherhood. She appears to be the most calm and gracious and loving mother on the planet. Plus, her family's outfits are matching, and their home is gorgeous— and every single square on her Instagram account is a pretty shade of pink accented with flowers and a flowy font.

Or maybe I come across a mother who lives on a farm from what appears to be another era with her perfect family. And every day she bakes her own sourdough bread and milks the cow and churns her own butter and homeschools her six children and wears floral dresses and smiles a lot and keeps vases of wildflowers on their old farmhouse table.

Or perhaps I find a mother who lives "tiny" and documents all these amazing travels with her husband and children who are always, *always* laughing as they explore nature. And apparently the whole family has been across the entire world, which is made obvious by endless pictures of breathtaking natural scenes.

And suddenly, I'm annoyed. And a little jealous. And slightly panicked. I begin looking at my own ordinary life, thinking, *What am I even doing? What is my "thing," anyway? Do I even have a "thing"? Why aren't we more nice? Why haven't we moved to a farm? Why aren't we laughing more? Could I pull off a long floral dress? And when are we going to get these kids to all fifty states? Why does it feel like we are so utterly ordinary?*

Sigh.

The truth is, I really, really try to be a good and kind and patient and loving mother. But usually by about 10 a.m., I'm pretty worn out and short on patience because no one is listening and the milk is gone (again) and one kid stepped in dog poop and the cat puked on the floor and "OH CRAP, WE MISSED *ANOTHER* ZOOM MEETING!!!"

The idea of raising chickens and canning food from our garden and cooking everything from scratch and going off the grid and living a life like the good ol' days sounds super romantic. Sometimes I wish it could be me! But then my mind wanders to my teenagers and their love of Little Caesars pizza and their basketball teams and Fortnite and Nerf guns and all their friends and popping some microwave popcorn for a marathon viewing of *The Goldbergs*. Plus, I'm well aware we can barely drive *across town* with all seven of us in one car without everybody bickering and bothering each other and throwing elbows and asking when we're going to be there and complaining about how cramped it is and "Why can't I sit in the front?" or "Mom, he's looking at me!" until I'm ready to scream. I'm pretty sure we're not going to be traveling the globe in a tiny home any time soon.

Our rugs are tattered and worn. Our corners are cluttered and dirty. We argue. A lot! And I always intend to cook at home with vegetables and a side salad, but probably three nights a week we either order in fast food or make cereal and toast. I am constantly telling myself tomorrow is the day I'll get it all together . . . but then life happens.

It turns out we *are* so utterly ordinary.

And these little people I'm raising are human. Real humans with personalities and preferences and quirks and opinions and challenges all their own. Just like their parents. It turns out there are actual people living in this house. People who make mistakes and ask for forgiveness. People who stumble and fall and stand up and try again. People who have good days and bad days and all the days in between. People who are trying every day to learn and change and grow up the best way they know how. People who mostly just need a loving family who believes in them.

Real life and real motherhood are a lot different from what I expected. Real life is hard. And mostly ordinary. And exhausting and messy and gritty. These kids? They bicker a lot. They fight and whine and argue and talk back. And they really stink at listening. They don't want to eat a fancy dinner with vegetables and a side salad. And all of it makes a mother want to yell sometimes (or possibly even break her own finger).

I wish I could say that, after sixteen years of parenting, I have it all figured out. I wish I could say I never mess up or get it wrong or fall flat on my face. I wish I could say I'm the perfect mother, and all my days are beautiful and Pinterest-worthy. But the truth is, I'm not. Not even close.

Day after day I mess up in a million ways. I struggle to find the right school or the right team or the right level of responsibility. I struggle to know when to step in to help my kids or when to step out and allow for natural consequences. I struggle to find a patient and loving response to my teenager's rolling eyes. I just . . . struggle. And the guilt runs deep. Sometimes it's hard to carry all that guilt and then scroll through other people's carefully curated lives. I don't think a filter would even begin to help mine!

I wish it wasn't so messy. This life. And motherhood.

But you know, I find myself squinting my eyes a lot. And when I look up and look around and squint my eyes, the picture distorts just enough that I can see our very messy, very ordinary little life in a very *real* way. Because sometimes my kids play the "Wild Bull" game on the living room floor with everyone screaming and running and taking turns. The pillows go flying and the noise level is ridiculous and inevitably someone gets hurt, but boy do they have a good time! And sometimes we sit down as a family to eat a deliciously nutritious dinner

I wish it wasn't so messy. This life. And motherhood.

of cereal and toast, giving our high/low for the day. Eventually one brother says something obnoxious, and everyone laughs, and occasionally milk streams out of another brother's nose. So I sop it up with a paper towel and store that precious little memory away. And sometimes my sweet middle boy, James, leans over to me in his quiet way and says, "Uh, Mom? Can we play?" while the rest of the house is distracted or busy, so we play endless hands of UNO at our worn kitchen table. And sometimes we order pizza on Friday night while my teenagers play Fortnite with a bunch of friends. For hours. We've become a "no screen-time limits on Friday night" kind of family. And sometimes Lizzy sings the "Our Father" in her sweet little voice at church while wearing her Sunday dress and holding hands with her big brothers. And I want to cry because my motherhood and our ordinary life is so ridiculously beautiful.

God always knew motherhood would be hard, messy work. He understood exactly the ways I would struggle. He realized I would mess up and get it wrong and fall down and keep trying and love fiercely and never, ever give up. Maybe He always meant for me to do motherhood *un*-curated. As an imperfect human attempting to raise other imperfect little humans in a world full of trials and tragedies. Not searching for perfection as a mom, but striving only to seek Him in the middle of the mess. Realizing a little more every day my complete dependence on Him.

And maybe . . . just maybe . . .

He chose *me* for messy motherhood. Because He knows that despite my imperfections and the countless ways I'll get it *all* wrong, I'm just the right mom for the job.

TWENTY-FOUR

not another *should*

For a while I wanted to blame my mother for my mess. I'm not sure why, but for some reason I gave my dad a free pass. I think it's because for the longest time my mother had everything I needed. She was safe and warm and loving. She rocked me and sang to me and let me sleep on the floor next to her bed for as long as I needed to (which was until sometime in the third grade). And she held my little hand every night until I fell asleep.

The problem was, eventually I started growing up. And she stopped having the magic to fix my problems. Never mind that I was so busy pretending and hiding and propping things up and achieving and attempting to fill all the holes by myself that I forgot to tell her I ever had any.

And never mind that in her own life she'd grown up in a house with ten children and lost her father to a heart attack when he was only in his early forties, leaving their family to fend for themselves. The oldest children worked in a nursing home kitchen to make ends meet, and my mother had a baby of her own by the age of sixteen.

So maybe it was my grandma's fault? Oh, wait. She grew up in Germany during World War II and remembers running back into the house from the bomb shelter to feel around in the dark for the youngest sibling's bottle. She moved to the United States speaking very little English while already raising two babies of her own. I guess we *all* have problems.

My job is to provide support and unconditional love along the way while God works out the details.

Now *I* am the mother. And Lizzy believes I am her everything. She is by my side nearly every moment of every day. She even wants me to keep her company while she poops. We play this little game where she laughs and says, "You and me are like bacon and eggs," and her little eyes squinch up as her face breaks into a dimpled smile. Then she turns to me. "Your turn, Momma. Now you do one." So I say, "Yep. You and me are like peanut butter and jelly!" And she laughs.

But I long to lean over and say, "No, honey. We're not. I'm so sorry you won't have everything you need. Not from me, anyway. I'll walk beside you for as long as I can, sweetheart. But Jesus will be with you . . . always. And I promise, honey. I promise I'll cheer like crazy as you go out and find your *own* way. With Him."

That's the thing I have to remember.

My children each have their own personal path. And for now, our paths intersect. But the truth is, they know better than I do what the journey along their path will look like as time goes on. And only God knows the destination. My job is to provide support and unconditional love along the way while God works out the details.

I guess I'm still letting that sink in, because when my son says, "Mom, I don't think I'm going to be Catholic when I grow up. I don't think I'll go to church at all, actually. I don't even know if I believe in God. Not the way our church puts it, anyway," my insides begin to feel hot and panicky. Because wasn't that one of my main jobs?

I remember perching in front of the baby swing when he was seven days old. Crying. Staring at his beautiful face. Unable to peel my eyes away. Feeling this immense weight as his mother to protect him. I remember feeling quite sure that if a pack of wolves entered our living room at that very moment and threatened my baby boy, I would be ready and able to fight them off in an instant. He was mine. *MINE.* And I was created to protect him.

I am his mother.

The wolves never came, so I just kept staring. I whispered aloud, "God, I don't ever want him to feel sad. Or scared. Or lonely. Or afraid. Or helpless. Or small. Please help me protect him. I want my baby to have a happy life."

It was such a funny thing to say. Because wouldn't having a mother who shields him from *everything*—fights off all his wolves for him, prevents him from feeling *anything* but goodness, happiness, and peace—make him feel a little helpless? And small? I mean, don't we learn who we are by making our own way? And how to be strong by fighting our own battles?

It's all so confusing.

And I still do it. I constantly want to shield my children from life. I wish somehow that my own story, my own wisdom, and all the lessons I've learned through my own pain and struggle and failures these last forty-plus years would be enough for my children. Enough to make them believe. Enough to make them run right to Jesus. And never question. I've hoped my children would take all my hard-earned faith as their own with open hearts.

For the longest time, I wished they could avoid life's pain somehow. Maybe if I tried hard enough, pushed hard enough, arranged the pieces just so. Maybe if I was a good enough mother or a perfect enough parent. Maybe if I held their little hands until they fell asleep . . . or forever. Maybe then my children could avoid feeling even the smallest shred of pain.

Because isn't that my job? To teach them? Protect them? Shield them? Leave them without any doubts or questions?

It hurts too much to think otherwise, doesn't it? It hurts too much to imagine my children are actual human beings living their own beautifully complicated and ordinary lives. Walking their own path. Setting out on their own journey with Christ. It hurts too much to acknowledge that I get to walk beside them for such a short little while.

The hardest part of my own faith is trusting God with my greatest treasures. Believing my children are His. *HIS.* And trusting He will seek my children. Trusting He will lead them wherever they are meant to go.

I know He came after me. I believe He saved my husband from the depths of despair. I believe He rescued our marriage. Chased after us into the darkness. So I'm not sure why it's so hard for me to believe this will happen for my children. I must trust that God will go after them too. Then I can hold my children more loosely, knowing that releasing my grip is just another testament to my faith.

As their mother, I'm realizing it will be so painful to watch. Because deep down I know my children's paths will include hard lessons. Pain. Suffering. Despair. Hopelessness. Failure. Surrender. I know that even as God chases closely behind His one lost sheep, He allows that sheep to wander in the darkness for a while.

What's funny is, my son says things like, "Mom, I don't know if I believe in all that stuff," and I panic a little. But this teeny piece of me completely understands where he's coming from. Can I tell you something?

I struggle a lot with my religion. I struggle with all the rules. Sometimes I find myself overly concerned about what the other parishioners think of me. And what my priest thinks of me. And how godly my little family appears to everyone else. I wonder constantly if I'm doing it right. I wonder if I'm good enough. I wonder if I have a handle on all the rules set before me. And do those rules really determine my salvation?

Maybe all those rules are part of what my teenager is struggling with too. And I wonder sometimes if we are all missing the point. Am I missing the point?

Honestly, the God I've come to know cares less about my rule-following and more about my heart. He cares about how I love Him. He cares about how I love other people. I believe more than anything else, He wants me to share my life with Him. He wants me to know Him. And He wants to know me in return. Intimately. And I truly believe He wants me to share Him and His love with the world.

The truth is, my kids have a bunch of *should*s they attend to every day. Things like standing in line and raising their hands and taking turns and sharing and completing assignments and being here or there on time and doing their chores and running hard at basketball practice and all the other *should*s of the world. I don't want Jesus to be another one. I don't want Jesus to be just another *should* in their lives. I want my children to *want* Jesus.

And because I want them to want Jesus, I make room for breaks from church when they need it. I am okay with the occasional Sunday morning at home in our pajamas when my kids feel like they're drowning in the hustle and bustle and rules and regulations and *should*s of life. When they tell me they just need a break from all the striving and doing and needing to be somewhere on time.

I want my kids to *want* Jesus.

And because I want them to want Jesus, I listen to their fears and doubts and let them know I have about a million of my own. I share my own encounters with God and my own beliefs and pray with them and for them, but then do my best to avoid shoving the rules and church regulations and all *my* beliefs down their little throats.

I want my kids to *want* Jesus.

And because I want them to want Jesus, I try to give real responses when they ask the tough questions. Oftentimes, that means I respond with, "I don't know." Because some of it is confusing. And *I don't know.* There are parts of the Bible and our church beliefs that don't make a lot of sense to me. So many things I just don't understand. I am still learning. And I tell them so. I tell my kids how I struggle. And wonder. And worry. I tell them I will probably get it wrong in a million ways, but I keep trying. And I will keep trying. Forever.

I want my kids to *want* Jesus.

And because I want them to want Jesus, I do my best to tell them what I *do* know. So I tell them I know God is love. And Jesus is His son. And above all, we are called to love Jesus and other people because we belong to Him. He loves me. And He loves them. And He loves *all* of us with a love we can't possibly understand.

I tell them I *do* know that when I walked into our little church up the road for the very first time, the priest recognized us as new members of the congregation and asked us to stand up as everyone clapped and welcomed us. Then the talented woman who was leading the music that day played "Amazing Grace" on the acoustic guitar, and on our way out, the priest hugged us all with such enthusiasm that I have never felt so at home anywhere in my whole life. So I keep coming back.

I want my kids to *want* Jesus.

And because I want them to want Jesus, I plant all the seeds and water them as best I can and lead by example and love others and pray for my children every single day. But mostly I try to *get out of the way* so they can find their own path toward Jesus. And I have to believe Jesus will find them. He's already walking beside them. He has a plan. The *best* plan. So I need to let go of my own.

I have to remember that most of the rules and standards and man-made traditions and many parts about organized religion don't matter in the long run, really. *Love* does. And I just have to keep showing up. Keep raising my hand. Keep loving as best I can with all my human imperfections. And all my failures. And all my misunderstandings.

I have to remember Jesus didn't care much about perfection, anyway. Or rules—not the world's rules, anyway. He liked to hang out with the sick and poor and dying and desperate. The prostitutes and lepers and outcasts. The people who were doing it wrong. I mostly read over and over in the Bible, these were His people—not the righteous who pretended to have it all figured out, not the ones with all the rules and heavy yokes of *doing it right*, but the ones the world deemed unworthy. The ordinary, everyday screw-ups.

Kind of like me. And my kids, I guess.

I want my kids to *want* Jesus.

And because I want them to want Jesus, I will never stop showing up. To church. To marriage. To mothering. To writing. To doctoring. To loving. To learning. To living my utterly ordinary life. And even when I do it all wrong, I will keep raising my hand. Keep raising my voice. Keep shouting out loud, "Jesus, choose me!"

I hope my kids will too.

Because I want my kids to *want* Jesus as much as I do. Jesus, show us the way.

Whether you turn to the right or to the left, your ears will hear a voice behind you, saying, "This is the way; walk in it."

Isaiah 30:21

TWENTY-FIVE

a new season

The thing they always warned me about is happening . . . my kids are actually growing up.

When I imagined motherhood, I envisioned chubby, dimpled cheeks and toothless grins and that sound of a solid pat on a tiny, diapered bottom. Forever. But suddenly, when these bigger boys of mine aren't playing basketball, they are mostly sitting like lumps and eating chips and staring at the TV or playing Fortnite. They get annoyed by anything we do as a family. They hate the music I play in the car. And they have very little tolerance for their younger siblings.

Oh, and they stink.

They eat me out of house and home and leave a dirty ring around the bathtub and forget to pick up their dirty laundry *every single night.* They complain about chores. They complain about screen-time limits. They complain about family outings. "Mom, why can't I just stay home?" They complain there is nothing to eat. They complain about going to church. They complain about nearly everything these days!

And nothing is fair.

When I tell my teen to put his phone away, he says something like, "Why can't we just be a normal family?" because apparently, we are the only parents to set limits. And it's hard. Parenting is just so *hard*.

If I'm being perfectly honest, most of the time I have no idea what I'm doing. Do I step in? Do I step out? Do I move out of the way of natural consequences? Do I intervene and advocate? Do I give more responsibility? Less? Does he need to talk? Should I bite my tongue? What about a hug? Is that what he needs? Was that the right thing to say??

I just *don't know*.

In some ways, it was simpler when they were little. Diapers and nap times and teething and terrible-twos and never sleeping through the night and potty-training. It all seemed hard at the time. I was soooo tired. And I always assumed it would get easier. For years I heard moms of older kids say things like, "You think that's hard, just wait till . . ." and I would smile and nod but inwardly respond with rationalizations: *At least you are getting a full night of sleep. At least he can dress himself and poop in the toilet. At least he doesn't throw himself on the floor and pitch a fit in Target.*

But they were right. Even when kids are older, parenting is still so hard. A different hard. Maybe harder!

Eye rolls and arguing and constant boundary pushing and silent treatments and endless screens and dropping them off for an afternoon with friends along with a few silent prayers . . . *God, please keep them safe.*

Sometimes I mourn the loss of my babies. I mourn the loss of those fun and wild and hilarious little boys. Where did they go? I remember how they wanted mohawks one summer. And how they were always shirtless and barefoot. I remember how adorable it was when they lost their two front teeth. And, of course, how much they loved their momma!

One minute ago, my Eli was a little boy with dimples and a wide smile. He begged me to play LEGO for hours and always said he wanted to marry me when he grew up. Then I blinked, and now he is fourteen. *Fourteen!* A full-blown teenager!! Now he can be obnoxious. Some days he runs his sassy mouth and rolls his eyes and picks fights with his siblings as his form of play. I don't remember the last time he played LEGO because all he wants to do now is play video games or bounce the basketball around the house. Sometimes I wonder where my little boy went. Is he really going to follow in the footsteps of his older brother? Is he really going to grow up?

And then sometimes I panic as anxious thoughts push their way into my brain. *When was the last time I pushed him on the swings? Was it the backyard swings? Or the park? How old was he that last time? Did I give him an underdog? Did he ask me one last time but I was too busy picking up dog poop so I absentmindedly replied, "Just pump your legs," and he never asked me again?*

Sometimes I want to cry over this. Sometimes I *do* cry over this.

But then I remember to look for the beauty. I try to remind myself this is what is supposed to happen. My kids are *supposed* to grow up! And even though this new stage is different and frustrating and weird, it is absolutely lovely too.

I've discovered this new thing called The Front Seat. Suddenly, the little boy who was buckled in a car seat in the back for so long is big enough to sit in the front seat of the car. And every evening after school I drive him *everywhere*. Basketball practice and soccer games and late nights with friends. So nearly every single day I have this one-on-one time with my boy. He fiddles with the radio and turns it up way too loud. He chews all my gum. He tells me stories about school or friends or Fortnite, and I notice how those dimples flash as he gives me that same wide smile. If I'm really lucky, sometimes a good song comes on, so we sing together at the top of our lungs, and he doesn't roll his eyes or think I'm annoying at all.

Sometimes I want to cry over this. Sometimes I *do* cry over this.

Turns out, this season is lovely too. Different lovely. Maybe lovelier!

I have *two* teenagers now. None of my kids is wearing diapers, and it's a whole new season at the Albertson house. This is the season for cheering from the sidelines for the boys who tower over me at Saturday night basketball games. This is the season for watching *SNL* together on the couch or sharing funny (if not slightly inappropriate) memes. This is the season for Fortnite and phones and fast-food drive-through and "Hey, Mom, guess what?" and more food and laundry than I can possibly keep up with.

In this season, the big kids can watch the little kids while I go out for a bit. I can go to the gym or grocery store alone! I can make a list of chores and divvy them out to all the family members, leaving me with one measly little mountain of laundry to fold. And while it may not be perfect, my house looks relatively clean, and I'm not sweaty and exhausted at all. Now when I cook dinner, they eat! Enchiladas or barbeque pork sandwiches or chili or fish tacos or pretty much *anything* I put on the table is snarfed down in record time. These boys are hungry basically every single second. And they eat it all! They ask what's for dinner and exclaim "YES!" when I tell them sloppy joes. They even thank me. They *thank me* for making dinner.

In many ways, this season is even better than pushing babies on the swings because every single day I realize a little more what amazing people they are all becoming. The little babies I once knew are right in front of me, but somehow these beautiful *new* people are emerging too.

In this season, already the good memories of young motherhood far outweigh the bad, and I only remember sweet baby sighs and itty-bitty sneezes and the wonderful smell from the tops of their heads and baby cooing conversations and first laughs and how adorable Isaiah was in his monkey costume on that first Halloween.

Yes, I cry at Johnson's baby commercials. Yes, I gaze wistfully at the pregnant momma and her toddler at Target. And yes, I fight the urge to reach out and squeeze every baby I see. I understand, now, all the well-meaning older ladies who told me over and over to "enjoy every moment." And I am remembering all of it through slightly rose-colored glasses.

But honestly?

No one ever really told me what a gift it would be to watch my kids *actually grow up*. No one mentioned how beautiful it is to know a little person on his very first day and watch him become a confident young man right before my very eyes.

It is lovely.

What a lovely surprise to find myself talking and laughing with my whole heart next to me in the front seat of the car on the way to basketball. I just smile ear to ear because despite the hard, it is all so beautiful too—smell and all!

You know, I'm beginning to think this is how *life* is going to go. Things will inevitably change, so we'll panic and believe the best parts are over. We'll cry and mourn the passing of yet another stage. But then we'll be surprised again and again at the next breathtakingly beautiful moment to come along. What a gift.

This ordinary life is filled with the loveliest surprises.

TWENTY-SIX

i never knew

There's a lot of beauty in ordinary things. Isn't that kind of
the point?

—Pam Halpert, *The Office*

Dear Dan,

On our wedding day I had no idea who we would become.

I didn't know we would grow up together. And older together. I didn't know I'd grow rounder and saggier, and you
would become bald and bearded. I didn't know I would find
myself looking over at you all these years later and still catch
my breath sometimes, marveling at how handsome you are.
You're so distinguished in your forties!

I had no idea after your second stay in rehab, when you said
you were ready to try again at marriage and love and family
and life, you were actually going to *show up*. And keep showing
up over and over every single day. To work and marriage and
fatherhood and coaching and helping and loving and *life*. Sometimes I'm awestruck by the way you live your life. If integrity

had a little picture next to it in the dictionary, it would be your face. And sometimes I can't help thinking to myself, *He's such a better PERSON than I am. How did I get so lucky?*

It used to be, when you were very, very sick and our marriage was very, very broken, I had to imagine you as a little boy. A child. A baby your mother kissed and cuddled on her lap. Because for a while there, I had so much trouble loving the man you had become. Broken. And sad. And angry. And self-deprecating. And selfish. And lost. My eyes could only see the lies and pain. I could only feel how much you were hurting yourself and our family—and me. So the only way I could love you for a while was by picturing you as a child. And by trying to remind myself every day that you were, indeed, *His* child. A child of God. I had to remind myself there was a person inside that broken shell whom God still loved to infinity. No matter what. But honestly? I didn't know the scared, sad, broken little boy I loved would grow up to be the man I'm married to today.

> *It's clear to me God uses broken people. He repairs their hearts. He stitches them back together, and as He does so, He adds a little something extra.*

It's clear to me God uses broken people. He repairs their hearts. He stitches them back together, and as He does so, He adds a little something extra. I can see it in the way you live your life. I can see it in the way you work so hard. And in the way you love even *harder*. Week after week you give of your time and your money and your patience and your resources. You give to me and our kids and your colleagues at work and all those kids on our boys' basketball teams as you cart them around every night across the world to practice and home again (for four million teams that you also coach). You give.

And you *love*.

I certainly didn't expect we would love one another infinitely more after almost twenty years than we did on our wedding day. I don't love my babies any more today than I did on their very first day. My love for them has always been so full, so complete, so inherent, so final. But somehow, with marriage—with *you*—it's different. Because now when we wake up in the morning and kiss each other good-bye to go about our days, or when we give each other a look across the noisy dinner table, or as we lay together in our big king-sized bed at night, there are more than twenty-five years of memories right there between us. And I love you *more* today than I did in the beginning. So much more than I ever thought possible. I truly didn't know it could ever be this way. It's another of life's lovely surprises.

And I never guessed we'd raise five children. I always assumed you'd be a good dad, but I couldn't really imagine how amazing it would be to watch you raise our children into godly young people as you somehow manage to be firm and stern and real and soft and tender all at the same time. Somehow, I always pictured our life together raising little boys. Wild and loud and raucous. But I didn't know we'd have a surprise little girl at the caboose (even though I think we both sort of always *knew*). And I couldn't possibly imagine the incredible gentleness she would bring to your already so very tender heart. I adore watching you with our baby girl.

I love what a sap you are at Johnson's baby commercials or how your eyes tear up at every kindergarten Christmas program. It's so fun to raise our children with you by my side. Thank you for knowing when to step in to give me a break. Or when to give me some applause. Or when to give me a Sunday morning to myself. Or forever letting me know we're in this *together*. This is my very favorite thing—doing all of this with you! Life just keeps getting better, doesn't it?

Some people really do spend their whole lives together, and after nearly twenty years of marriage, we're still here. You love to cook, and I love to bake. You throw a load in the washer, and I make sure it gets to the dryer. You coach, and I cheer. I understand you like to sleep in on the weekends, and you know we can start that movie after the kids are in bed but that nine times out of ten, I'll be asleep on the couch halfway through. I quickly wipe down the kitchen every night, but when it's your turn, you deep-clean it. And every single night we pass one another in the hall as we take turns tucking in kids room to room to room. Nothing makes you happier than an afternoon trail-run in the woods, and nothing makes me happier than a bowl of chocolate peanut butter ice cream before bedtime. You understand I'm a Words of Affirmation girl, and I know you're a Physical Touch kind of guy (plus, who knew sex would keep getting better too? Lucky us!).

Somewhere along the way we stopped trying to change one another. We stopped keeping track and stopped keeping score and decided to be on the same team. Team Marriage! Now we're just two people growing up and growing old and raising kids and attempting to do this messy, ordinary life together. We're partners. Two parts, *loving* with our whole hearts.

And I love this story. Our story. I wouldn't change a single day. Not a single moment, not even the very hardest ones. Our story happened just like this for a reason. On purpose. And if I could sit down to write my own version, I would write it exactly as it played out. Heartbreak. Pain. Failure. Redemption. And incredible, unfailing *love*. Ours is a true love story.

How many times have our eyes met? Across the room. Across the tops of our kids' heads. Right in the middle of one of those tender life moments through our tears. And I know we are both thinking the same thing. *We almost missed this. We almost missed ALL of this. We almost walked away from this beautiful family. And three of our five amazing children very nearly never came into being. This family—this beautiful, ordinary life we are living—was almost completely lost.*

Our life certainly isn't perfect. Really, this might be all there ever is. This house. This marriage. This family. Us. I'll probably never lose those last ten pounds I'm always complaining about. And I'll probably never figure out a laundry system that doesn't result in piles of laundry, everywhere. We'll probably never find the perfect balance between working and parenting and marriage and coaching and friends and self-care. And we might always struggle along, just doing our best. Enjoying what we can. Messing up in all the worst ways. Apologizing, forgiving, trying again. Laughing and loving all the way.

But really, *this* is the life I prayed for all along and is exactly what He always had planned. We didn't miss it. I am so grateful to live this good, hard, ordinary life—my one precious, beautiful life—with you.

I love you.

Life is amazing. And then it's awful. And then it's amazing again. And in between the amazing and the awful it's ordinary and mundane and routine. Breathe in the amazing, hold on through the awful, and relax and exhale during the ordinary. That's just living heartbreaking, soul-healing, amazing, awful, ordinary life. And it's breathtakingly beautiful.

—L. R. Knost[1]

let go

I was never a regular churchgoer growing up. I mostly attended Mass on Easter and Christmas with my family dressed in fancy clothes; a tradition I carried forward into my early years of marriage.

But despite my record of haphazard church attendance, whenever life's pain or loneliness settled in my soul, I found myself drawn back to those old, familiar pews with those old, familiar prayers and all my favorite songs. And one lonely Sunday morning, many years before any of the beautiful family life I'm living today, I found myself at church. On this particular day, I couldn't remember ever feeling lonelier. I don't remember why. A fight? More bad news about my husband? My hormones? Who knows? But whatever it was, the unforgettable imprint of my inextricable loneliness remains.

I knelt to pray that morning with my hands clasped and my eyes tightly closed in a desperate attempt to keep the tears from streaming. I hoped so fervently that someone might notice me and reach out. Someone. Anyone. I needed a hug. A look. A hand on my arm. A kind word. Just the smallest bit of human connection. But it never came. Even among all those people gathered in one place to worship. And even as the Word flowed freely to my ears, reminding me over and over and over that He is always *right here*. Even then I felt utterly and completely alone.

After Communion, I let the Bread of Life dissolve on my tongue, leaving its comforting taste behind, and I knelt again as the music began to play. It was a song I'd heard a thousand times before, but this time the lyrics flowed over and through me. Words assuring me that God is with me, and I don't need to be afraid. Words reminding me that God has called me by name. Words urging me to let go and follow the One who claims me as His own, because the Lord our God *loves* me. And I am His.

I am His. I am His. I am His.

It echoed through my mind. Over and over and over. And somehow, even in my pain and loneliness, I started to sing that day. I sang through my cracked and wobbly voice. I sang with my trembling lips. I stumbled over the words and let the refrain wash over me as the tears I'd been fighting all morning came streaming down my cheeks and splashed onto the pages of the hymnal.

I am His. Of that I could be sure.

True, at the time I had no idea what would happen next. I had no idea if Dan and I would stay married. I had no idea if I would ever finish medical school. I had no idea if we might have a baby and start the family I always imagined, the beautiful family I prayed for. Everything felt so broken. And I had no idea what I was supposed to do next. But somehow, for just a few moments, I knew this one simple, certain truth:

I am His.

I don't remember the rest of that day. I don't remember exactly what happened after Mass. I guess I went home. But somehow in the days and weeks and years that followed, we did stay married. And somehow, I did finish medical school. And eventually, we did start a family. And, my goodness, how we struggled and stumbled through those next few years. A decade, actually. For the longest time everything felt so hard. So very broken.

I'm a regular churchgoer now. Week after week, I smile at the familiar faces I see around me. Sometimes I hug the man who lost his wife recently when he greets us at the door. I wave to the woman behind me whose hair is growing in so beautifully after the completion of her chemotherapy. Everywhere I turn, there are so many gestures of human connection in this place I've come to know and love.

On a recent Sunday morning, I found myself crammed into the pew, bumping shoulders with my ever-growing family. All seven of us. Together. Lizzy crawled around on the floor and over our legs and asked to be picked up, only to then ask to be put down. All the boys teased one another back and forth, and my second-grader clapped his little hand over his mouth to stifle his giggles. My sweet middle boy sat close to my shoulder in his quiet way. The oldest shot me a few dirty looks because the homily always

Everywhere I turn, there are so many gestures of human connection.

takes too long for his liking. And my bald and bearded, now-sober husband sat right there alongside me. Always beside me.

After Communion, the Bread of Life dissolved on my tongue as the music began to play, and suddenly there it was. *That song.* I've probably heard it a hundred times over these past few years. But today, for no special reason at all, I was transported back to so many years ago before *any* of this. Back to the day when I felt all alone in church. Back to the miserable, empty feeling of loneliness and my deep longing for connection, marriage, life, and family nestled in my heart.

Once again, my eyes filled with tears as I sang. And oh, how I sang on this day. I sang my little heart out through my cracked and wobbly voice and trembling lips as I let the familiar refrain wash over me. And on this morning in my chaotic, crowded pew, God leaned right over and gently pressed into my heart, *"You see, Mikala. I told you. Don't be afraid. You don't ever have to be afraid. I'm here. And you are Home. My child, you are mine. You just had to let go. And let me carry you."*

I didn't know it before. I wasn't listening. I couldn't see. But the truth is, I have always been His.

I am His. I am His. I am His.

Always and forever . . . I am His.

I wonder how many countless times we stumble through life searching—grabbing and clutching and tightening our fists. Desperately looking for answers to questions like *Is this right? Am I doing any of this right? Is this the answer?* When really, God's plan is already under way, and we just don't see. Maybe we need to let go to hang on. Maybe we need to break down to be whole. And maybe *this* life is a true love story after all. We just have to let go.

> So do not fear, for I am with you;
> do not be dismayed, for I am your God.
> I will strengthen you and help you;
> I will uphold you with my righteous right hand.
>
> Isaiah 41:10

TWENTY-EIGHT

he means me . . . and *you*

I struggle sometimes to comprehend He means *me*.

I believe God is good, yes. I believe He is listening. He answers our prayers. He forgives us. He loves us. Yes. I'm sure that's true. But somehow, I've always felt this applies to the world as a whole. The people. The masses. Perhaps everyone else.

But *me*?

It took me nearly forty years to even begin to understand and accept that He loves *me*. He knows what is best for *me*. He is listening to *me*. He answers *my* prayers (even if the answer is no). He has already forgiven *me*. He loves *me*.

ME. All imperfect and ordinary.

Now, what about you? Have you ever really thought about that? Have you ever really let this sink in? Really? Do you realize He means *you*?

Did you know that on the day you were born, He already knew who you were? Your name. What you would look like.

Where you were headed. *You.* You came blinking into the light, and He smiled with awe. At *you.*

You were already so beloved.

Did you know that as you learned to laugh and roll and crawl and walk and your personality emerged, He already knew who you were? What you liked. What you were good at. What made you happy or sad or angry or scared. And He was filled with joy at the mere sight, the presence, the being of *you.*

You were already so beloved.

Did you know that on the difficult day you never told anyone about because you were so ashamed, He was standing right there beside you? You weren't alone after all. You were never, *ever* alone. He held your hand. He held you safe in His arms. He hemmed you in behind and before. He never left you. *You.* And His heart ached at your heartache.

You were already so beloved.

Did you know as you struggled through school and peers and hard days and failure and insecurities, He was walking beside you? And as you celebrated and cheered your successes and became a little more yourself every day, He was cheering right alongside. He marveled at your every move, so proud. Of *you.*

You were already so beloved.

Did you know as you grew into an adult and started doing grown-up things like college and a career and marriage and parenting and buying homes and starting over and all the joy and pain and heartache and beauty of life and wondering if you are doing any of it right, He was there? He *is* there. Right beside you. Walking with you every step. Sometimes carrying you when it is just too hard to endure on your own. Always loving and smiling and encouraging and beaming. At *you.*

Because you are already so beloved.

Beloved.

From your very first day. Every single day. Today. And on every day to come. He is here right now. With *you.*

The mistake you made. The lie you told. That fear you carry. The dream you keep tucked away in the middle of your heart. He already knows.

What if you walked around every day believing He means *you?* Really and truly believing He knows *you.* Everything about you. Every word, every dream, every breath. What if you finally grasped how much He loves *you?* Every single piece. Every seemingly insignificant moment.

He means YOU.

From your very first day. Every single day. Today. And on every day to come. He is here right now. With you.

All those words in the Bible? They are for *you.* And His death on the cross? It was for *you.* God is so good. He is listening. He answers our prayers. He holds us tight. Even on our very worst days, we are forgiven. Already made perfect in His hands.

He loves us.

And that means *me.* And *you.*

We are forever and always so beloved.

> You have searched me LORD,
>   and you know me.
> You know when I sit and when I rise;
>   you perceive my thoughts from afar.
> You discern my going out and my lying down;
>   you are familiar with all my ways.
> Before a word is on my tongue
>   you, LORD, know it completely.
> You hem me in behind and before,
>   and you lay your hand upon me.

Such knowledge is too wonderful for me,
  too lofty for me to attain.

Where can I go from your spirit?
  Where can I flee from your presence?
If I go up to the heavens, you are there;
  if I make my bed in the depths, you are there.
If I rise on wings of the dawn,
  if I settle on the far side of the sea,
even there your hand will guide me,
  your right hand will hold me fast.
If I say, "Surely the darkness will hide me
  and the light become night around me,"
even the darkness will not be dark to you;
  the night will shine like the day,
  For darkness is as light to you.

For you created my inmost being;
  you knit me together in my mother's womb.
I praise you because I am fearfully and wonderfully
  made;
  your works are wonderful,
  I know that full well.

                              Psalm 139:1–14

on purpose

I always hated my body. Hated it for as long as I can remember, really. Ever since I became aware of how a woman is *supposed* to look: thin waist; full, curvy hips; large, perky breasts—and all scantily dressed in suggestive clothing. I'd seen movies and magazine pictures. And I stumbled over a few images as a child I'm sure weren't meant for my eyes. Plus, I'd been fondled and touched in that particular way early on, so I knew what it was all for. What it was all about.

As a kid, it was generally my custom to take off all my clothes and examine myself in the huge mirror above the bathroom sink for a few minutes before climbing into the shower. Naked, with the hot shower steaming up the room, I stared. Pulling and tugging and pinching and lifting. Turning and examining with such critical eyes. Wondering if I might ever possibly look like one of those images I saw in magazines. Wondering if I might ever feel beautiful.

I mostly just felt chubby and soft and greasy and awkward and roly-poly. I'd look over my chest and size things up and wonder when in the world my boobs would start to grow. So many of the other girls had them already. I'd cup my hands over my chest and look up with prayer, *God, I can't wait for my boobs to be THIS BIG.* Then I'd examine my inner thighs and grab at the flesh beginning to collect there. I'd turn sideways and look at my protruding tummy. I was getting so fat. *Am I going to be a fat girl? God, why?*

Then suddenly, one day in the middle of one of these naked examinations, as I turned sideways to look at my growing girth, my heart dropped, and I could feel the pit growing in my stomach once again. *What if I'm pregnant?*

Obviously, I had no idea how it worked. I hadn't even had a period yet and my sexual abuse had been *years* earlier. But I did know I had been fondled and touched and kissed. I did know a boy's penis had touched my private parts at some point and now I had a "huge" tummy. So, what if?

What would I say? What would I tell my parents? What if this hurt their feelings? What if they were mad at me for never telling them the truth? What if they didn't believe me? What would I tell my friends? What about school? Can a twelve-year-old raise a baby? Would I still be able to play soccer?

I worried for months. I was so relieved when nothing happened. And that year my waist grew thin, and my hips became a little more round and shapely, and I sprouted some boobs, and later that spring, in the middle of Spanish class . . . I started my period.

There was a small window during college when I did feel beautiful. Over the summer before my junior year, I put myself on a "no carb" diet. But not in a healthy way. I ate eggs and hot dogs and cheese and sausage patties and hamburgers without the bun and peanut butter with cream cheese or cashews as my dessert. I ran often. And far. Even obsessively. And when

I returned to college in the fall, I'd lost at least ten pounds. Maybe fifteen. And suddenly it felt like people noticed me. Suddenly I was beautiful. I saw it in the way I was accepted into new groups of friends. I saw it in the way the boys' eyes followed my body as I walked to class. Never mind I never ate fruits or vegetables or bread. Never mind I never drank milk or participated in ice cream socials or birthday parties. Cake?? I don't think so. Never mind I sometimes restricted all day long just to wolf down a double cheeseburger (without the bun, of course) before heading out to the bars at night (where I usually chose vodka because, no carbs!). And never mind I occasionally broke the "diet" and made myself throw up in the bathroom.

I was beautiful. I felt beautiful. And I didn't need to pinch at the extra fat or flesh around my thighs or circling my middle. It wasn't there. All my hard work was paying off.

Even now, all these years later, after marriage and medical school and babies, I'm finding it difficult to break that train of thought. I'm finding it hard to push away the idea that an apple or a banana or a simple slice of toast is "bad." And that when I eat a sandwich with carrots and chips, I've "ruined" my eating for the day. Usually when this happens, I just eat more. Might as well have a few chocolate chip cookies too! The day is already ruined!

Having five babies meant gaining forty pounds and then losing thirty-five pounds five times. And it means that my waist is no longer thin. My breasts no longer perky. My thighs coated with a lining of soft flesh that rubs together when I walk.

And I struggle. I struggle to feel beautiful. When I undress before my shower, sometimes I still can't stop my gaze from lingering on my soft roly-poly body as I wonder, *How can my husband still think I'm sexy? I don't look anything like the women I see on TV or social media. Again, God, why?*

A few years ago, I had a dream. It was one of those early morning dreams when consciousness seems to move in and out. I felt so aware I was dreaming, but still the images came. And I remember it all so vividly. It seemed so real.

I found myself picked up in two enormous hands. God's hands. Two hands just like the painting of *The Creation of Adam* hanging on the wall above my couch as a child. And I was naked in His hands. Like a newborn. His child.

God touched and stroked and caressed every inch of my body. It was the most intimate dream I've ever had without feeling even the slightest bit sexual. And as He touched on each little square of flesh, I felt Him whispering,

"My darling. I see you hating this body every day, but don't you know I made you on purpose? Don't you realize I created you just like this for a reason?

"And don't you know, sweetheart, when I imagined you, I chose squinchy, hazel-colored eyes that would crinkle at the edges whenever you laugh? Don't you realize it was I who touched your right cheek with my index finger, leaving one dimple to perfectly punctuate your beautiful smile?

"And my dear, this belly now decorated with silvery white lines was created to carry those five beautiful babies I know you love with all your heart. And your breasts up above fed and nurtured each one. Darling, don't you remember how those beautiful babies would pause in the middle of nursing to lock eyes with you and love you and smile?

"And don't you know I gave you broad shoulders and strong arms to carry your babies for all these years, and to offer hugs and plant flowers and carry groceries and walk the dog and do all the other tasks of this world along with strong legs to walk and dance and play and run?

"Can you understand I gave you a heart to LOVE people, and this love of words to HELP people? And don't you know,

sweetheart, I chose ALL of it? Your auburn hair. Your thin lips. Your white teeth. Your high cheekbones. Your long middle toes.

"I'm so sorry anyone ever hurt you. That was never, ever what I intended when I created you as my beautiful child. My masterpiece. Please know, while it hurt you so deeply, it absolutely broke my heart. I was there. I held you close. And I promise, you were never alone.

"My child, I want you to know that when I look at you, I only see LOVE. And in my eyes, no matter how you look or how old you grow or whatever your weight, I truly believe you are BEAUTIFUL. You are the most beautiful thing I've ever seen, actually. You are mine. And all of it—every piece, every part, every quality, every single cell—was created by me. My darling, you are so very ON PURPOSE."

I woke up with tears in my eyes. So ridiculously loved. And so very much on purpose.

I don't want to miss a single moment because I'm afraid. Afraid I'm not thin enough. Or I don't look right. Or I'm not perfect enough somehow.

I still struggle sometimes. Oftentimes, actually. With wishing I were just a little smaller. Just a little lighter. Just a little smoother. Just a little tighter.

But I realize a little more every day that this body, *my body*, was created by Him. And it may not be perfect by the world's standards, but it is so very on purpose. And it's the body I've been given to love my husband and to raise my children and to live this life. My one precious, beautiful life. What a gift! I don't want to miss a single moment because I'm afraid. Afraid I'm not thin enough. Or I don't look right. Or I'm not perfect enough somehow.

I think Anne Lamott said it best,

Oh my God, what if you wake up some day, and you're 65, or 75, and you never got your memoir or novel written; or you didn't go swimming in warm pools and oceans all those years because your thighs were jiggly and you had a nice big comfortable tummy; or you were just so strung out on perfectionism and people-pleasing that you forgot to have a big juicy creative life, of imagination and radical silliness and staring off into space like when you were a kid? It's going to break your heart. Don't let this happen.[1]

I won't let this happen.

I will give my one beautiful body plenty of healthy fruits and vegetables and nuts and grains and protein. And feed it plenty of milk and cheese and water. And my daily vitamin. I will run a few days a week to stay strong. And make time to rest it at night.

I will hold my babies and dance in the kitchen and chase after them laughing as I try to steal the soccer ball in the backyard. I will wear the swimsuit and jump in the pool after them, laughing and splashing. I will walk the beach with the sand in my toes where the water glides up to meet me, washing over my feet. I will celebrate birthdays with ice cream and cake and attempt to bake cream puffs on a random summer morning and spend Sunday afternoons mixing up a batch of chocolate chip cookies that we'll all eat warm from the oven. I will stop worrying (so much) about my nice, big, comfortable tummy.

My body is a gift. This life is a gift. And I'm done hating the gift I've been given. Every day I will care for it the best way I can. I will love it the best way I know how. I will set an example of love for the little girl who watches me and calls me Momma. And I will try to remember every morning as I gaze into the mirror, to look for all the *beauty* amid my imperfections.

I was created by my Creator with love . . . and I will remember, every day that He thinks my body is beautiful. And I am beautiful. The most beautiful thing He has ever seen.

And you know something? I believe everyone else is too. We are *all* the most beautiful thing He has ever seen.

THIRTY

the messy middle

Plans are made. Plans come apart. New delights or tragedies
pop up in their place. And nothing human or divine will map
out this life, this life that has been more painful than I could
have imagined. More beautiful than I could have imagined.

—Kate Bowler, *Everything Happens For a Reason*

It seems like this should be an *after* story, right? And I should
have it all figured out now, right? You know, before . . . after.

Because once upon a time I thought my sole purpose on
earth was to live the most perfect life possible (or at least *appear*
perfect). And once upon a time my marriage was crumbling
as I struggled to control a husband who was hooked on drugs
and alcohol and in and out of rehab. And once upon a time I
had two little boys under three and a family practice residency
that demanded way more of my time and energy than I could
possibly give. And once upon a time I was drowning in life . . .
sinking further into the depths of despair with no way out. I
was lonely. And lost. And scared. And alone.

Once upon a time I felt broken. And life was broken. That was *before*. So this should be the *after*.

Because today my husband is clean and sober for thirteen years, and our marriage is stronger than I ever could have imagined. Today I've let go of my plan for a big, fancy house and all of life's extravagances. I've stopped chasing after perfection. Today I know: "perfect" is *pretend*. And today I spend my days raising babies and working part time and enjoying what I can in this beautiful, ordinary life I've been blessed with.

This must be happily ever after, right? And life should be easy now. Better. Beautiful. Happy. Right??

And I suppose it is—kind of. Mostly. Except for when it's not.

The truth is, most of life still feels like the middle of my story. The *messy* middle.

My days can still feel hard. Marriage is still hard. Motherhood is still hard. This new stage with teenagers is definitely hard. A pandemic is hard. The living of *life* is still so very hard. And often I'm lonely. And lost. And scared. And feeling alone. I'm still a little broken, it seems.

Every day I wonder if I'm doing any of this whole thing right. *Is this right? Why is it all so hard? Why do I still struggle? All my prayers have been answered. Maybe not exactly the way I envisioned, but in many ways, this story I'm living is even better than what I prayed for. This is better than what I had planned. And I should just be happy now. Right?*

Then, time and again, the world leans over and whispers tauntingly in my ear, *"There IS more, you know. More money to be made. More success to be had. More people to please. More accolades. More achievements. More awards. There's more. You should do more. Work harder. Strive. Achieve. You are capable of so much more. You should BE MORE."*

And I can't stop myself from wondering as those lies settle in my brain for a few moments, *Is the world right? Is this enough? Should I be . . . MORE?*

But then I pray. I sit quietly. I allow myself to be still, and I listen to God's whispers pressing in all around. In the stillness, the world's lies fall away once again because I remember true greatness comes through Jesus. It turns out I don't need recognition or praise from the world, because He tells me I am enough. I am loved and worthy right now. Just like this. Today. Even right here in the middle of an imperfect and ordinary life with Jesus leading my path and filling my days. And every single morning and over and over throughout the day, I will make the decision to serve exactly as He asks me to: with *love*.

Most mornings I switch laundry from the washer to the dryer and load the dirty breakfast dishes. I play outside with my kids and push little bottoms in swings. I pluck ripe, red cherry tomatoes from our overgrown garden. Then at lunch someone inevitably spills their milk, so I click around the kitchen in jeans and a T-shirt with my flip-flops, and I tuck a few loose strands of hair from my messy ponytail behind my ear as I wipe up the mess. And somehow, in the middle of an ordinary day, my mind drifts back to that calm, quiet, ordinary woman in my office so many years ago. And I realize with relief, *I so obviously love this life.*

These days I am getting better at placing my expectations into the right hands. Instead of placing my expectations on the people in my life or the applause of the outside world, I'm placing all my expectations with Jesus. Instead of seeking happiness or more stuff or more awards or a perfect life or more popularity or people's accolades or belonging, I'm realizing that with Jesus, I can expect so much more—real love, tenderness and mercy, and a beautiful, unending grace. With Him I can expect a fullness of life I never imagined. And with Him to carry my load, I can expect to be surprised in all the best and messiest of ways.

Though He never promises life will be easy.

The world will always dictate how to live, if we let it. The world will fill us with lies about how to have more and do more and be more. Speeding us up and sending us into a frenzy in order to achieve . . . something. Always chasing after yet another thing we're not even sure we want. Something always just out of reach.

We're told Real Life will begin out there in the future somewhere. Someday. Maybe once we finish school or get married or start a family. Maybe once we buy our dream house or start our new job or get that promotion. Perhaps when the kids are all potty-trained or once everyone is in school or if we finally shed those last ten pounds or tick a few things off our bucket list.

But it's not true.

Because when we slow down and stop chasing . . . when we let go of doing *all* the things because we've been told over and over that's what

> *When we somehow tune out all the noise of the world and listen to God's whispers . . . we can find the life God truly intended for each of us to live.*

we're *supposed to do* . . . when we sit in the stillness and silence . . . when we somehow tune out all the noise of the world and listen to God's whispers on the breeze, it is then we begin to realize what we really love, and discover who it is we really are. It's then we can find the life God truly intended for each of us to live. Real, messy, beautiful. And it's right here.

Real Life is right now.

Life is ordinary, mostly. And it's in these quiet, ordinary moments I hear Him whispering ever so gently, *"It's here, Mikala. I'm right here."*

In the ordinary I've found such profound beauty and grace, love, a bit of stillness, and gratitude. And it feels like I've been let in on a little secret: Life happens in the ordinary! This beautiful life of love and connection and grace. Of deep relationship and belonging. It's *right here.*

My heart feels like it might burst, and I want to cry out loud with gratitude, because I almost missed all of this! Always so busy striving and attaining and achieving. Forever pressing forward. Listening to the world and all those lies and the never-ending *should*s. Chasing perfection and forever falling short. My race for perfection almost stripped it all away.

But now I know.

"Perfect" is *pretend.* The world is a liar. And I didn't miss it. Ordinary found me. The very real, very messy, very beautiful life God truly intended for me to live is right here. In the ordinary.

So . . . here I stand. Exactly as I am. Plain and mostly unspectacular. With a million flaws and doubts and all my limitations. With two feet planted right in the middle of an ordinary life. I'm learning to be more present now and content with what I have and how I look. I'm learning to love *who* I actually am. And I'm more grounded somehow. My faith has changed and continues to grow. I understand a bit more what it means to know Jesus and to be loved by Him and to live rooted in His ridiculous grace.

My life isn't perfect. It's quite messy, actually. And I'm okay with that. I'm realizing a little more all the time, I'm not looking for an *after* story. Not really. That's not how it's supposed to go, because my story is still unfolding. My story is still being told. This is *today's* story.

Lovely. Mundane. Ordinary. Beautiful.

And we are all right in the middle of it with new characters, different plot twists, and further challenges. This isn't our final destination. One day, at the end of all our days, we'll experience the true *after*. With Him. He is the *after* story. He is our happily ever after.

And all of this?

This is the beautiful, messy middle.

Just for today I will be unafraid. Especially I will not be afraid to enjoy what is beautiful and to believe that as I give to the world, so the world will give to me.[1]

it will be beautiful

The only thing that was ever wrong with me was my belief that there was something wrong with me.

—Glennon Doyle, *Untamed*

It wasn't long after I visited my grandfather in the hospital and forgave my flawed, recovering husband and began to let go of my deeply held resentments over life's injustices, that I began working very, very hard to radically love and accept *me*.

I am sitting next to the little girl in the purple swimsuit at one of those picnic tables on the covered porch. She is happily swinging one leg back and forth with a flip-flop dangling precariously from her toes while sipping on Pepsi from an icy cold can. I notice a few boxes stacked next to us on the ground. And I am struck by how incredibly small and beautiful she is as I lightly rifle through the contents of the first box hanging open at the top. I quickly realize our stories are there. Our truth. Some consist of words scrawled in messy shorthand on a random scrap. Some are made of pages and pages all typed neatly and bound in a fancy folder. Others are just crumpled and yellowed bits of paper containing only a word or two, tossed in on top or jammed into the corners. All of it is there—all of *us*. Our life stories are jumbled together there in a stack of boxes.

I watch as she sits across from me completely unaware of the demands of the world, happily sipping away as a drop of condensation dribbles down the side of the can. She catches it up with her tongue and laughs. Then, with sudden inexplicable sadness, that familiar pit forms in my stomach as I realize how I've hurt her. Bullied her. I think back to all those times I spat angry judgmental words her way. How I ridiculed and rebuked her. Hated her, even.

How did you let this happen? Again? Look at you. You're awkward and ugly. You're chubby and soft. You're stupid and sluggish and slow. Why don't you try a little harder? Push a little harder? Strive a little harder? When are you ever going to learn? Come on, catch up! You'll never make it. I don't think anyone can love you anyway. You're broken.

And every single time she fell or faltered, instead of gently helping her to her feet, dusting her off, and grabbing her hand as if to say, "It's okay, sweetheart. Let's try again. We can do it together!" I would point and laugh and chide her with cutting, hateful remarks: "I'm not even surprised. See? I told you. One day everyone is going to figure it out . . . you don't belong. And you're right, you know. There *is* something very wrong with you."

But I look at her now. So small. So sweet. So innocent. I can't pull my eyes away from her little frame. That little face. It is like I understand for the very first time, she is *none* of those things. Not even close.

She is lovely and brilliant. She is treasured and adored. Wholly and completely beloved. So worthy of love. How could

I *ever* treat her that way? How could I be so cruel? How? My breath catches a little in my throat as I stare. And with fresh, new eyes I suddenly realize, *My God, she's so very beautiful.*

Then my gaze drifts back down to those boxes. I realize with sadness all the things this little girl will soon struggle through. All those days. And years. All that pain. So many moments of disappointment and loneliness. Moments she will feel afraid and alone and unsure. All the times she will look in the mirror and wonder why she can't just do better. Be better. And thinner and smarter and more beautiful. And . . . perfect, somehow.

I want to warn her. I want to tell her when to run and what to shout. I want to show her how to stand up for herself. And believe in herself. I want to teach her how to *"I love you. And He does too. Nothing else matters."* avoid any pain. And more than anything, I want to tell her how beautiful she is. I long to tell her about mountains and sunsets and the intoxicating smell from the tops of her babies' heads. I want to reassure her that in this life we *do* have pain, but there will be fun and laughter and happiness and connection. I want to tell her there *will be* hard times, but there will be beauty too. THERE WILL BE BEAUTY TOO!!!

But I don't yell out any of that. Instead, I lower myself down and crawl around to her side of the table. I grip her lightly by the shoulders and gently bring myself up face to face. And stare. I stare into her amazing hazel-green eyes. I stare for as long as it takes for this beautiful little girl to recognize herself. I stare for as long as it takes for her to realize the life in her eyes is reflected in mine. I stare until she realizes . . . it's *me*.

Then very, very softly I whisper, "I love you, you know. And He does too. Nothing else matters. We don't *ever* have to be alone. Not ever. And this life? All this beauty?? It's for *us*, honey. I promise. I know it's hard. Life is filled with so much pain. But there will be beauty too."

She is a little taken aback at first. Then her eyes well up with tears as she breaks my gaze and looks away. Ashamed. So I lift her chin lightly with my index finger until our eyes meet again, and I say, "I love you, sweetheart. I'm sorry if I *ever* let you think I didn't love you. You are precious, and I love you. I always will. There is *nothing* wrong with you. Not a single thing. And I won't ever hurt you again. I love you."

Then her amazing little face spreads into a wide smile. Her eyes crinkle slightly at the edges, and the dimple in her right cheek flashes when she laughs. "That's what I've wanted all along!" she replies as she hops up from the table. Then she dances and twirls away across the grass as I just watch from my knees. And smile. Suddenly, I notice for the very first time as Jesus stands and follows quickly behind her. I didn't realize He'd been sitting there at the table with us. Listening. And loving us. But now He follows after her as she disappears across the grass and out of sight.

I open my mouth and attempt to call out, but He turns and puts up a hand to quiet my storm of questions and doubts and instructions. Then, ever so gently, He reassures me, "I am here. I will be with her every step of the way. Why do you doubt? Don't worry, my child. Remember? It *will* be beautiful." And with a smile, He turns to follow her.

I smile again then too, and my heart feels so completely at peace. My gaze falls upon all those boxes. *Our* boxes. I lift the lid of the very first box and begin pulling out our stories, one by one. I take each of our lovely, painful, messy, heartachingly beautiful life stories out of the boxes and smooth the crumpled edges and straighten all the bits and scraps into piles and begin shuffling them into some semblance of order.

I smile and laugh and cry as I reread each story. My stories. *Our* stories. One after another. I am reminded once again how incredible it all is. *LIFE*. Isn't life beautiful?

I'm not really sure where I ever got the idea that I'm supposed to *know* who I am and what I want and where I'm going and what I'm good at and all the rest—but I was wrong. I was wrong all this time. The truth is, I'm in my forties now and I still don't fully know. I just discover her a little more all the time. And sometimes I get into something for a bit or become someone for a while only to discover sometime later, I'm not her anymore. So I start all over again to find her.

The thing is, we never get to a place of Here It Is. We never truly *arrive* because we are always and forever in a state of *becoming*. More ourselves. Someone fresh and new every day.

There is never an *arriving*.

There is only a *becoming*.

I lived so many years of my life assuming I must be doing it wrong because I never seemed to *arrive* anywhere. Not for long, anyway. I looked outside myself a lot. I listened to parents and teachers and grown-ups and friends and authorities and whichever crowd happened to be in the Circle at the time. But it's a lie. All of that narrative is a lie.

I really can't do it wrong. This is my *life*. And now I understand so completely, there has never been a single thing wrong with me all this time. I'm just *becoming*. Becoming a wife. A doctor. A mother. A Christian. A sister. A friend. A writer. A daughter. A philanthropist. A runner. A neighbor. A child of God. A woman.

A human.

Me.

A little more *me* all the time. Every day, bit by bit. Becoming.

Sometimes it's right and sometimes it's not. Sometimes it lasts and sometimes it doesn't. Sometimes it feels good and beautiful and whole. And sometimes it hurts like hell. *Becoming* is all these things. All our experiences. All our moments. All the stories we've kept hidden away in boxes. Somehow, we grow and change and fail and flounder and cry and laugh and learn and fall and fight. And we are held forever in His ridiculous grace . . . as we emerge. Brand-new over and over again. Always and forever, so *beloved*.

I stop, then, in the middle of shuffling through all those bits and scraps of our life stories. And I stare after where the two of them disappeared across the grass—the precious little-girl me with Jesus following close behind. And I wonder for just a moment if she will be okay. *Will she really be okay?* I suppose she *must* be okay if He is right there by her side.

I wonder quietly for a moment if she will ever tell. *Will she ever share our stories?* Then I realize with such incredible pride . . . she just did.

And He was right. Life really *is* beautiful.

For as long as I'm living and breathing, I'm becoming someone new. I'm becoming me. I'm becoming free. And so, my friend, are *you*. Life is sure to be messy. And mostly ordinary after all. But we find so much beauty right here amid the rubble.

acknowledgments

Thank you to the One who whispers. The One who treats me with tender hands as He leads me through this troubled life. The One who calls me "sweetheart" and "darling" and only ever watches me through an adoring smile because He loves me so much. Always. No matter what. Thank you for your patience. I know I still get it wrong most of the time. It's so comforting to know you'll wait for me forever. Thank you for whispering in my ear whenever I'm in need, *"This is the way, walk in it."* You've never, ever led me astray. I love you with my whole heart.

So much love to my mom and dad. You were the best parents I could ask for growing up. You loved and served and coached and drove and cooked and cheered and gave me every single thing I could ever need. I know it was hard, and I'm so grateful for your sacrifices.

For my sister, Cherie, your constant support and faithful prayers mean the world to me. I'm so glad I'm finally growing up so we can be the same age and raise all these kids and compare notes and live our lives together. You are such a gift to me!

Rosie, thank you for loving me like your daughter. Thank you for sending giant boxes of random fun things in the mail because you know I'd never buy them for myself. Thank you for praying unceasingly. I guess you can't call yourself only a Boy Mom anymore!

Thank you to my girlfriends, near and far. You know who you are. Life wouldn't be the same without you, my dear friends, and I am forever grateful. Thank you for listening to my same boring stories. Thank you for letting me struggle through the same ridiculous dilemmas. Thank you for your free phone therapy (Amy, I'm looking at you!) as we both speed along to basketball practice a thousand miles apart. I am so grateful for your understanding that I am a slow learner and a long talker. Thank you for loving me anyway. Thank you for knowing exactly the right time to call or text or reach out or send me a Birth Day cake. When I think back to any of the moments I remember laughing the hardest in my life, one of you was probably the culprit. Thank you for making my life so fun!!

Thank you to all the truth-tellers and story-keepers. To the writers who've gone before me, your writing changed everything. I've cried a million times and whispered aloud to the room, "YES!" I wouldn't be writing if it weren't for all of you. Thank you. Oh, and Glennon and Jen, I'll be ready for chips and salsa on the porch to celebrate this new book whichever evening works for you!! LMK.

Katie Dilse, you were a hidden treasure in my life, and I *know* God put you in my path for a reason. Thank you for presenting me with that imaginary diploma on the plane. Somehow it started everything. Please visit me the next time you are in Utah.

Thank you to Lisa Leshaw for only ever telling me how wonderful and amazing I am. You are the best cheerleader of all time, and I just know you walk around all day blessing the hearts of every single person who crosses your path. What a gift and a calling you have! Thank you for reading my little book when it was just a glimmer of an idea. Thank you for reminding me I have a story to tell. And that my story matters. Thank you for telling me every single day I am a Glorious Warrior. You, my friend, are the Queen of the Warriors, and I love you to pieces.

For Mrs. Allberry, the world's spunkiest Spanish teacher, I know you are smiling down at me right now. And cheering. I can just hear you clapping your hands and clicking your heels. I keep your book with the sweet letter sent all the way from heaven on my nightstand. I read it cover to cover in one sitting and all I could think was, *She's the bravest person I know!* That's the very first time I believed I would write a book. I wanted to be brave and live this beautiful life just like you! I wish I could send you a copy.

For my other most influential teachers:

- Mr. Hammond, I can almost imagine your tiny red cursive writing all over the pages of this book, "Beautiful alliteration, Mikala." You taught me all about passive voice. And how to eliminate the use of the word *that*. I wish I could send a copy to you too! I think you'd be so proud.
- Mr. Oltmans, you were right. The B in AP calculus that nearly broke my heart really didn't matter after all. Thank you for knowing I needed that little failure more than I needed to be valedictorian in high school.
- Dr. Kelter, thank you for reassuring me one failing grade on my first college chemistry test wouldn't ruin my semester score. And thank you for the gigantic smiley face you drew inside the 106% I got on the next test, and for cheering so loud right in front of the other two hundred students when you handed it to me. Sometimes I still need to be treated like a kindergartener.
- Dr. Hill, you knew my hard story during medical school and treated me *exactly* the same. "Your husband is in

rehab? Again?? So sorry, now get to work." It was just what I needed. And I know you didn't have to give Dan so many chances. But I think you always saw exactly what I saw in him. And we were both right . . . he is a brilliant physician now! Once upon a time you told me casually you wouldn't hesitate to practice medicine in a clinic with me because I am a good doctor. And your passing comment remains one of the highest compliments I've ever received. I've always admired you so.

Dear patients, thank you for sharing your life with me. You teach me to love and help me to heal with every single one of your stories. Kindra, you continue to be a blessing in my life. I'm so grateful. Practicing medicine is truly a gift . . . for me.

Thank you to all the people who make up Her View From Home, my internet home. Girls, you are the BEST!! Four years ago, when I got the email accepting my publication on Her View, I cried. I bet we all did! And the most wonderful and unexpected blessing from this entire writing journey has been *you*. Leslie, look what you've created! To Angela and all my Writer Peeps, what would I do without your daily doses of reality, your beautiful spirits, and your loving hearts? And Jenny Albers, I'm not sure how I might possibly survive life without our constant conversations about anything and absolutely EVERYTHING (including cat videos, of course). You are my favorite! You guys, I never imagined I'd come to know and love "internet people" the way I love all of you. We talk almost daily. We cry over one another's stories. We love and encourage and pray for each other every step of the way. Writing. Motherhood. Marriage. Life. I'm so grateful I get to do this with *all* of you!

Thank you to my literary agent, Blythe Daniel, for taking a chance on representing my book and leading me through the process. To Whitney Childers for helping me with all things technology. To Bethany House, my editors, and *all* the people working on each component part, I am forever grateful. And to all those who signed up for the *Ordinary on Purpose* book launch team, I appreciate you. (I really can't believe I just wrote that sentence. Because, a book? Really?? Who would've ever thought?!)

And you, dear readers. I'm so grateful for all of *you*. Once upon a time I started a blog and I had thirty-nine readers. I didn't imagine it would ever become anything more than writing a few words here and there and sharing it with my aunts and cousins (who have always been my very BEST supporters!). But then it grew. I wrote. People started showing up. And the fun part is, I write to encourage others, but so often my readers encourage *me* and reach out to *me* and support *me*. I have a love/hate relationship with social media. But you guys? My readers? You are the BEST! I appreciate all of you! Thank you for coming along on this journey and doing life beside me.

Finally, thank you, thank you, thank you to my little family. You are my people. And you are the *very best part* of my story. Hands down. Isaiah, Eli, James, Luke, and Lizzy, I adore each of you. You are the loves of my life. I can't believe I get to be your mom! Thank you for being amazing kids. Watching you grow is the greatest blessing of my life. I thank God for you every single day. And Dan, I can't believe this is our life now, can you? Isn't it fun? Not perfect. Nope. But more than I ever could have dreamed. Love and fun and laughter and chaos and slammed doors and clogged toilets and shoes everywhere and tiny hugs and half our life spent in the car on the way to basketball practice and more noise than we can handle. We are exhausted. But so *FULL*. I wouldn't change a single thing. This is the beautiful, messy, ordinary life I always wanted. And you, dear husband, are my dream. I'm so grateful I get to live every day of my life with my very best friend. I love you.

notes

This Ordinary Life

1. See Matthew 11:28–30.

Chapter 1 Widen the Circle

1. Shauna Niequist, *Present Over Perfect: Leaving Behind Frantic for a Simpler, More Soulful Way of Living* (Grand Rapids, MI: Zondervan, 2016), 27.
2. Niequist, *Present Over Perfect*, 28.

Chapter 6 My Unraveling

1. Brené Brown, *The Gifts of Imperfection: Let Go of Who You Think You're Supposed to Be and Embrace Who You Are* (Center City, MN: Hazelden Publishing, 2010), xii–xiii.

Chapter 8 Queen Martyr

1. *How Al-Anon Works for Families & Friends of Alcoholics* (Al-Anon Family Groups, 1995), 35–36.

Chapter 10 Brokenhearted

1. Henri J. M. Nouwen, *Reaching Out: The Three Movements of the Spiritual Life* (New York: Doubleday, 1975), 9.

Chapter 11 I Want Ordinary

1. Jen Hatmaker, *Of Mess and Moxie: Wrangling Delight Out of This Wild and Glorious Life* (Nashville: Nelson Books, 2017), xx.

Chapter 15 Making Amends

1. Addiction is an illness that affects not only the addict but everyone in its path. Al-Anon is a fellowship of family and friends of those suffering from addiction, who come together to provide strength and hope through shared experience in order to bring solutions to common problems. You can find more information about Al-Anon, including online or printed materials, as well as meeting locations near you, at https://al-anon.org/.

If you are in an abusive relationship and need help, know that you are not alone, and resources are available. Two amazing online, discreet resources are thehotline.org and wannatalkaboutit.com.

Chapter 16 Forgiveness

1. Jen Hatmaker, *Of Mess and Moxie*, 195.

Chapter 17 Dr. Stay-at-Home Mom

1. Jennie Allen, *Anything: The Prayer That Unlocked My God and My Soul* (Nashville: W Publishing, 2011), 165.

Chapter 22 This Perfect Stranger

1. Glennon Doyle, *Carry On, Warrior: The Power of Embracing Your Messy, Beautiful Life* (New York: Scribner, 2013), 25.
2. Elizabeth Gilbert, *Big Magic: Creative Living Beyond Fear* (New York: Riverhead Books, 2015), 12.

Chapter 26 I Never Knew

1. A 2015 Facebook post cites the source as an unpublished work, *Inhumanity: Letters from the Trenches*, L. R. Knost—Little Hearts/Gentle Parenting Resources, Facebook, September 5, 2015, https://www.facebook.com/littleheartsbooks/photos/quote-from-one-of-my-moms-upcoming-books-inhumanity-letters-from-the-trenches-sh/994074393956498/.

Chapter 29 On Purpose

1. Anne Lamott, Facebook post, April 8, 2015 at 4:31 p.m., https://m.face book.com/AnneLamott/posts/662177577245222.

Chapter 31 It Will Be Beautiful

1. *Prayer for Today*, Al-Anon Family Group Headquarters, Inc.

MIKALA ALBERTSON is a family practice doctor turned mostly stay-at-home mom who is passionate about all things beautiful and ordinary. She and her husband of twenty years live just outside of Salt Lake City, Utah, and together they raise their five children who range from ages sixteen to five.

You'll find her most days in jeans and a T-shirt at the neighborhood grocery store stocking up on food, or at home attempting to keep laundry from overtaking the house. She loves hiking in the mountains, reading, and writing, but her main hobbies include picking up dirty socks and driving her kids from basketball practice to soccer games and back again.

She loves to tell the *truth*. And she writes about motherhood and marriage and all things imperfect and ordinary on her blog **Ordinaryonpurpose.com**, where she'd love to have you follow along!

Mikala's greatest hope for writing is to give you permission . . . permission to release your grip on all the should-do's and have-to's and comparisons and "I'm not measuring up" and just be free to *live your life*. This one. The life God has planned for you, however imperfect. In this body with these relationships in this house at this job with these parents and these circumstances. This plain, old, good, hard, ordinary life . . . your *one* beautiful life. Join her. And be Ordinary on Purpose!

This is her first published book.

YOU CAN FIND MIKALA ON SOCIAL MEDIA AT

　f　https://www.facebook.com/ordinaryonpurpose.blog

　◎　https://www.instagram.com/ordinaryonpurpose/